MOHAMMAD NASEEM
Director Al-Markaz - Incharge Tarbiyah

*In the name of God,
the Merciful, the Compassionate*

Marriage in Islam

A Manual by

MUHAMMAD ABDUL-RAUF

Al-Saadawi
Publications

P.O. Box: 4059
Alexandria, VA 22303
Tel: (703) 329-6333
Fax: (703) 329-8052

© Copyright by Muhammad Abdul-Rauf

U.S.A.
Al-Saadawi Publications
P.O. Box 4059
Alexandria, VA 22303
Tel: (703) 329-6333
Fax: (703) 329-8052

LEBANON
Al-Saadawi Publications
P.O. Box 135788
Sakiat Al Janzir, Vienna Bldg., Vienna St.
Beirut, Lebanon
Tel: 860-189, 807-779

Library of Congress Catalog Card number: 75-186483

MARRIAGE IN ISLAM
ISBN # 1-881963-48-9

First printing, 1972
Second printing, 1974
Third printing, 1977
Fourth printing, 1981
Fifth printing, 1993
Sixth printing, 1995

Printed in the USA

To My Wife

Contents

The manuscript of this book was prepared during the year 1969 when I was working as the director and Imam of the Islamic Cultural Center of New York. By then I had been involved in conducting marriage ceremonies for hundreds of couples of all nationalities, and became familiar with the anxiety, the fear, and the questions, marrying couples usually ask. I had likewise been involved in cases of conjugal problems, counseling, and settling of domestic quarrels. Some good friends also urged that I should write a manual for the benefit of Muslims in North America who were exposed to the dangers of the then raging so called sexual revolution and its coarse, lustful manifestations.

The book was intended to serve as a guide to young Muslim couples, contemplating marriage and as a brief source material for Muslim families living in a climate saturated with values and norms inconsistent with their cherished traditions.

The launching of the work in 1972 earned instant wide popularity, and it was reviewed by prestigious Americans and international news media publications. Subsequently, four reprints of the book appeared. Now that the American publisher has wound up his business, Mr. Safa Al-Saadawi of Al Saadawi Pubilications has graciously offered to reproduce the work. I am grateful to brother Safa Al-Saadawi and wish him and his publishing firm continued success and prosperity.

Muhammad Abdul Rauf

Bathesda, Maryland, USA
10/20/1413 AH
4/12/1993 AC

Preface

DURING the past five years which I have thus far spent in the United States serving as director of the Islamic Center of New York, in which capacity I have been regarded as a clergyman of the faith of Islam, I have united in marriage almost five-hundred couples, mostly of the Muslim faith. In this experience I have often been disturbed by the couples' inadequate knowledge of the significance of the important event in which they were about to be involved. When they called to see me about the arrangements for the ceremony, they appeared to be unnecessarily nervous and apprehensive, and asked about minute trivial details which seemed to them to be of momentous consequence. I therefore felt the need for a simple, comprehensive manual that would help prospective spouses in what they were about to embark upon. I hope that this book will be found both instructive and reassuring, and that it will contribute to the greater stability and happiness of Muslim homes in America.

I was also urged by one of my American Muslim friends, for whom I have high regard, to write a monograph on the subject of sex from the point of view of Islam. He said, "You have to remember the great difference between you, who were born a Muslim, and people like me who adopted Islam at an advanced age. Up to the time we made our choice, we had been exposed only to Western literature, much of which"—as he put it—"commercializes sex in a filthy manner, exploiting the low animal instincts in man, producing now and then best sellers." He revealed to me some of the abominable practices described in these works, and added that many Muslim sisters and brothers often inquire of him concerning an Islamic guide on sex. He remarked that the absence of such a guide was an appalling omission. My friend appealed to me to fill this gap and strongly advised me to treat the matter with unrestrained frankness and clarity.

And thus I was caught between my personal inclination, which shuns even the use of the term sex, and this compelling need. The latter consideration, I felt, was indeed more justifiable.

It is in response to this appeal and to this compelling need that the subject of sex relations is discussed in this book wherever it is appropriate.

Although I address myself primarily to Muslims, I hope that the publication of this manual, which is likely to reach the hands of many of my fellow men who do not profess the Muslim faith, may create more understanding about our religion, the faith of Islam, which is hardly known in the West and yet is closely akin to Judaism and Christianity. In the current turmoil of male-female relationships in Western society, a manual on the institution of marriage in Islam should be both interesting and enlightening.

January, 1971   M.A-R.

Chapter One

Is Marriage Desirable?

Marriage in Islam is strongly recommended on religious, moral, social, psychological and physiological grounds.

SCRIPTURE AND TRADITION

Many Koranic and traditional texts can be quoted in which the practice of marriage is urged. The following is a sampling of some Koranic texts.

The Koran, which Muslims believe to be the word of God, reads:

> *And marry those among you who are single. . . . If they are needy, God will make them free from want out of His grace. [XXIV, 32]*

> *And He it is Who has created man from water; then He has made for him blood-relationship and marriage-relationship. And thy Lord is ever Powerful. [XXV, 54]*

> *One of His signs is this: that He has created mates for you from yourselves that you might find quiet of mind in*

them, and He put between you love and compassion. Surely there are signs in this for a people who reflect. [XXX,21]

In the context of praising the prophets preceding the Prophet Muhammad, the Koran reads:

And surely We sent Messengers before thee and appointed for them wives and children. [XIII, 38]

And in praising the habits of good believers, it reads:

And those who say, "Our Lord, grant us in our wives and our offspring the joy of our eyes. . . ." [XXV, 74]

There are also many traditions ascribed to the Prophet Muhammad in which the practice of marriage is emphatically praised. The following are some of these traditions:

Marriage is my recommended custom. Whosoever turns away from my recommended custom is turning away from me.

Get married so you multiply. I shall indeed be proud of your multitude on the Day of Resurrection.

Get married, and do not divorce; indeed, divorce causes the Throne [of God] to shake!

O you young people, men and women! Whosoever can bear the burden of marriage let him or her get married. It [marriage] is indeed contentment to the eye and a protection to the modest parts.

When one is married, he secures half of his religion. So let him fear God in the other half.

ADVANTAGES

☞ PROCREATION

This is the paramount advantage of marriage; namely, to contribute through legitimate means to the continuity and preservation of the human race. The sexual urge serves the function of bringing the mates together for the fulfillment of this basic objective.

The procreational objective has four aspects: to fulfill the will of God; to seek the love of the Prophet Muhammad; to benefit from the prayer of the child; and to profit from its intercession on behalf of its parents.

Almighty God, in providing the male with intricate fertilizing organs and the female with a receptive fertile womb, is telling us in the most eloquent but voiceless language of the purpose of these provisions. To let them be idle is to ignore the divine wisdom written on these God-given instruments. Imagine a farmer who, although he is given a piece of fertile land, seeds and farming tools, just lets the land go to waste, the seeds rot and the tools rust. This farmer not only is a fool but is to be condemned for his wasteful and harmful indifference.

Procreation through marriage is also a means of seeking the pleasure of the Prophet Muhammad, peace and blessings be upon him, who is believed to be alive in his grave and to whom the deeds of the members of his nation are regularly presented. He has called upon his nation: "Marry, so your number increases." The practice of marriage is an answer to his call.

Prayer of a child is believed to be beneficial to his dead parent. The Prophet, peace be upon him says:

> *When the son of Adam dies, nothing would be of any more benefit to him except three things: a continuous charity, some useful knowledge he has left behind and a child who may pray for him.*

Should the child die early and the parents accept its loss as an act of God, without despair, it would be like a ticket to Paradise for them. The Prophet, prayers and peace be upon him, is related to have said:

> A child [who dies before reaching puberty] leads his parents to Paradise.

> A child will be brought [on the Day of Judgment] and told, "Get into Paradise." But he will stand reluctantly and angrily at its gate and say, "I am not going to enter Paradise without my parents." It will then be said, "Let his parents enter Paradise with him."

It is related that an unmarried man of good conduct who lived in the early past shouted when he was rising from sleep one morning, "Help me to get married! Help me to get married! Maybe God will give me a child who will be useful to me on the Day of Judgment." He was asked, "What has happened?" He said, "I dreamt that the Day of Judgment had come, and all mankind was raised and brought together in one place with the burning sun close over their heads. Everyone became very thirsty and I was dying of thirst. Suddenly, children appeared among us, lively and handsome, covered with protective light and carrying silver ewers and golden goblets. They offered drinks to some but left out most. When I stretched my hand to one of them and said, 'Give me to drink, I am exhausted because of thirst,' he said, 'You have no child among us.' I asked, 'Who are you?' He said, 'We are Muslim children; our parents lost us when we were young!'"

☞ FULFILLMENT OF THE NATURAL URGE

The sexual urge is perhaps the most powerful human inclination. It seems not to be an end in itself but a means to bring the mates together for the purpose of fertilization. Yet its fulfillment is the most enjoyable and absorbing of human experiences. Failure to fulfill this urge is likely to lead either to deviation or to maladjustment. Deviation is dishonorable and is strictly forbidden in Islam. Therefore, the Prophet, peace be upon him, calls upon youth, saying:

> *O you young people! Whoever of you can afford to get married, let him do so. Those who cannot afford it, let them practice fasting, as it may be a protection to them [against sin].*

It is believed that the intense pleasure of the climax of the sexual act, though short-lived, has the value of reminding the believers of the more durable and more perfect enjoyment that awaits them in Paradise. The experience should enhance their zeal to comply with divine teachings.

So the practice of marriage is the way to remove evil and protect against shameful failure. To try to suppress the sexual urge by other means, such as fasting, may succeed in preventing the eyes from looking at forbidden scenes and keeping the sexual organs away from committing heinous abominations; but there is no way of freeing the heart from engaging in meanest thoughts, pondering and dreaming of acts it craves for, even during the hallowed time of the performance of prayers. A person of any degree of respectability would never dare to speak openly of such mean thoughts to any creature, but he has no control over his mind to prevent it from roaming into these thoughts when he is addressing his Creator in prayers! Some exegetes say concerning the Koranic statement which reads, "And man is created weak" that the weakness is that man cannot afford to do without women. Some also say that two-thirds of man's wisdom is lost when his male organ becomes erect. Al-Junaid, one of the major founders of the Sufi movement, used to say, "The sexual act is as important to me as food." And thus a wife is food for the man and a measure for purifying his heart. Therefore the Prophet, peace and blessings be upon him, commanded that whenever a man sees a woman and feels attracted to her, he should go and release his urge with his own wife in order to remove the evil thoughts from his mind. The Prophet sometimes added, "His wife surely can offer as much as this woman does." He also forbade visiting women when husbands are away. It is related that Ibn 'Abbas, a cousin of the Prophet, once noticed a youth staying behind after a lecture he had given, when the other members of the audience had gone. When Ibn 'Abbas asked him about his problem, the reluctant youth complained that when he was overwhelmed by sexual excitement, he released himself by performing masturbation. Ibn 'Abbas was horrified and condemned the act, but said that the practice was less abominable than fornication.

It was because of fear of the dangers which might arise from an unfulfilled sexual urge that the early Muslims did not hesitate to rush to new marriage once they became widowed. Imam 'Ali, cousin and son-in-law of the Prophet, remarried on the seventh day of the death of his wife Fatimah.

☞ A HEALTHY RELAXATION

In marriage there is comfort to the soul, there is beauty to look at, there is company, and there is play and joking and relaxation, all of which relieve the heart from its burdens and make the mind better able to concentrate during prayers and worship. To be always serious and deprive the soul of its joy is boring to the heart and would blind it. Relaxing through the company of the spouse is healthy; and that is why the Koran describes the spouse as a source of mutual comfort. It is said that it is wise to divide one's time over three types of activities: worshipping the Lord, self-examination and entertainment of the heart. The Prophet, peace and blessings be upon him, used to say, "Two worldly things are beloved to me: women and perfume; but the light of my eye is in prayers." It is related that Al-Asma'i, an ancient Arab philologist, once encountered a beautiful Bedouin woman in the desert wearing a red dress and holding worry beads in her beautifully henna-dyed hand. Al-Asma'i remarked, "What a contrast!" meaning that the worry beads, a sign of deep religious devotion, and the henna dye in the hands, a popular cosmetic practice, did not go together. The beautiful righteous woman retorted poetically, "There is in me a devotion to God which I cannot neglect; but there must also be room for my heart and for my pleasure."

☞ A COMFORTABLE HOME

Marriage, moreover, provides cooperation in the household and greatly relieves one from worries. Spouses cooperate in the management of the house, in its upkeep, in cooking and washing, and so forth. And thus there will be more time for worship and seeking knowledge, and a climate conducive to concentration. It is therefore said that a righteous wife is not a wordly asset only; she is a sure way to success on the Day of Judgment. The Prophet, peace be upon him, says:

> *Seek to have a grateful heart, a sweet tongue and a believing, righteous wife who would help you in your endeavor to success on the Last Day.*

He also says:

> *If God loves a man, He gives him a righteous wife. If he looks at her, she pleases him; when he is with her, she is marvelous company; and when he is away, she observes conscientiously his rights, protecting his property and preserving her honor.*

☞ SOCIAL IMPORTANCE

Finally, by adding responsibilities upon the individual, marriage enhances his status in society and gives him an opportunity for training in bearing the hardships of life. Living with a spouse, a person of different inclinations and background, trains one in accommodating oneself to new experiences; each party helps the other in the exercise of the virtues of patience and forbearance. The responsibility of rearing children and the need to earn for their living are added meritorious aspects arising from marriage. Listen to the Prophet when he says:

A man will be rewarded for what he spends on his wife, even for putting a morsel of food into her mouth.

He also says:

Whoever performs his prayers correctly, and spends on his children in spite of his modest means, and does not speak ill against others will be in Paradise as close to me as these [two fingers of mine].

He also says:

Whosoever is given three daughters and spends on them and treats them well . . . surely God will reward him in Paradise.

DISADVANTAGES

There is no rose without thorns, and marriage is no exception. There is no relationship that modifies the mode of life of the individual or curtails the individual's freedom of action so suddenly or so profoundly as does marriage. Whether husband or wife, each has to take into account the reaction of the other party to whatever he or she may do.

☞ BURDENS AND RISKS

Upon marrying, the husband immediately carries the burden of the responsibility of his wife's welfare; and each birth brings forth more burdens. Sickness and other crises which may occur to his wife or to any of his children will be his own problems, and many of the things he would be able to enjoy by himself may fall outside his reach because of his domestic burden. And thus marriage brings him both hardships and deprivations.

The wife also, in addition to her husband's demands, becomes exposed to the burden of pregnancy, the pangs of birth, child care and the heavy task of nursing her husband and children when they fall sick. She has to do the shopping, prepare the daily meals, and wash and clean. She has also to pay regard to her husband's wishes and attitude. And so marriage for her is hard work and curtailment of her freedom.

Another disadvantage is the risk that marriage may prove to be a failure. If it is completely broken, then that is disastrous; and if it is maintained in spite of continuous troubles, life becomes hell. It is also likely in such a case of mutual tension that the parties behave unjustly to each other; and this will pile up sins for which they will deserve punishment on the Day of Judgment.

Moreover, the husband, in his search to satisfy the insatiable desires of an overambitious wife, or the needs of his children, may resort to corrupt or dishonest means, which would bring ruin to himself in this world and severe punishment in the life to come. The Koran remarks in this respect:

> *O you who believe, surely of your wives and your children there are enemies to you. So therefore beware of them.* *[LXIV, 14]*

Even if things proceed smoothly and comfortably in the household, the company of the wife and her attractions may excessively occupy the time and thought of her husband; and she may become too often engaged in amorous activities with him. It is said, "Wisdom is lost between the thighs of women."

☞ REFUTATION OF DISADVANTAGES

These are seeming but outweighed disadvantages. The burdened spouse is well compensated by the relief from the solitude and boredom of bachelorhood through the company of the other party and the children they both rear. Hardships they may suffer are worthy sacrifices in the interest of society. If everyone should run away from the responsibilities of marriage, mankind would degenerate, decline and ultimately disappear.

Engagement of the mind in the affairs of the household is not alien to the domain of divine worship. After all, the mind needs diversion and cannot easily be occupied in one type of work all the time.

The possibility of resorting to corrupt means to provide for domestic financial needs only arises with unscrupulous persons, married or otherwise; and marriage or need alone does not lead to corruption with conscientious, honest people. Married couples, however, should use their wisdom and manage their affairs within their means. They should not stretch their expenses beyond the income which they legitimately earn.

The possibility of failure in marriage is not a good cause for delay or reluctance. After all, there is a risk in every course of action in life, be it business, study, a journey or any other venture. If uncertainty of success were to debar us from venturing the risk, life would surely become paralyzed. It is only in courage and challenge that individuals and nations can aspire to glory. Moreover, if due care is exercised in picking one's spouse, the possibility of failure becomes rather remote.

Chapter Two

Steps to Be Taken in Marriage

SELECTION OF THE SPOUSE

Man, an intelligent social and moral being, cannot achieve the objectives of marriage through promiscuity. The young, who need long and watchful care, must be reared in a family setting containing a well-defined father and mother whose relationship is permanent, happy and very close. Promiscuity, moreover, is disruptive of social life and inconsistent with the dignity of man.

In making the selection of one's spouse, there are preferential and legal factors which have to be taken into account.

☞ PERSONAL PREFERENCES

Age, physical attraction, fertility and religious life have to be considered.

1. It is preferable, though not necessary, that the girl be a little younger than the boy. The wife is the receiving, protected party, and the husband is her protector and breadwinner. Male seniority in age is conducive to domestic harmony and greater peace.

2. It is also safer to ensure that the female party is of a degree of beauty satisfactory to her would-be groom; and that he is satisfactory in appearance to his prospective bride. Frustration in this respect may damage the chances of domestic

stability. Therefore it is strongly recommended that prior to proposal, boy and girl have a discreet opportunity to see each other. It would not be wise to depend, in the matter of selecting one's life partner, on the judgment of someone else. As has been said, this opportunity should be sought or arranged discreetly in order to avoid embarrassment should either party be disappointed.

Beyond the opportunity of this mutual observation, no private meeting should be allowed at all. The modern custom of dating is not only harmful and dangerous but also severely condemned and prohibited. A private meeting between a man and a woman who are strangers to each other, even if the man is a saint or a clergyman, is known as *khalwah,* and is not permissible. The Prophet, peace and blessings be upon him, said:

> *A man and a woman never meet alone except that Satan becomes their third party.*

However, the degree of beauty of the prospective bride should be given due consideration. The greater the beauty of the wife, the deeper her husband's enjoyment and satisfaction. It is said in this respect:

> *A desirous woman with wide black eyes, long black hair, a fair skin, who is of good conduct and who loves her husband and is devoted to him, is indeed one of the houri of Paradise.*

The Prophet also said:

> *The best of your women is the one who, when her husband looks at her, pleases him; when he commands her, she obeys him; and when he is away from her, she continues to have regard for him, protecting his wealth and preserving her honor.*

3. A factor that should also be taken into consideration is the potential fertility of the spouse, and this may be gathered

from the condition of her female married relatives, such as her mother or her elder sister. The Prophet, peace and blessings be upon him, said:

> *A child-bearing woman lacking in beauty is better than a beautiful but infertile one.*

4. Another important factor is the prospective mate's moral and religious attitude. A person of a righteous conscience inspires confidence and trust in the other party; and this is a sure way to peace and harmony in domestic life. The Prophet, peace be upon him, said:

> *A woman may be chosen for her wealth, or for her beauty, or for her nobility or for her religion. So choose a religious woman and hold fast to her. . . .*

A wife of easy morality would make life intolerable to her husband. Her manners would provoke his jealousy and arouse his doubts and distress his mind. She would cover him with shame in the eyes of others, who would despise him for his undue permissiveness; and their life would be hell if he tried to bring her under control. A man complained to the Prophet, "My wife never refuses a handshake." The Prophet advised him, "Part with her." The man said, "But I love her," and the Prophet retorted, "Then keep her."

A nagging or talkative woman is undesirable. It is related that a man of wisdom advised: "Avoid in marriage six categories of women: those who are mean; those who are of frequent complaint; those who are of divided hearts; those who are of an insatiable possessive eye; those who are too busy with the use of cosmetics; and those who are endowed with long tongues."

On the other hand, a would-be groom should be assessed more on the basis of his righteousness, as the Koran teaches, even if he may appear to be of poor means. The Koran reads:

> *If they are needy, God will make them free from want out of His grace.*

The girl is the weaker partner in marriage. It is therefore important to choose her spouse carefully. It is related that a man asked advice of Al-Hasan, the grandson of the Prophet, saying, "A number of men have asked for the hand of my daughter. To whom would you advise I should give her away?" Al-Hasan replied, "Give her to the one who fears God most. If he loves her, he will treat her very well. And if he does not love her, he will not be bad to her, out of fear of God."

The Prophet also said:

> Giving away a girl in marriage is almost like giving her to slavery. Therefore, be careful and see where you are depositing your daughter.

5. Virginity of the would-be wife is also more desirable, especially if it is the man's first experience with marriage. It is believed that a virgin will be a more loving and devoted wife. A woman with an earlier experience may find the new one of lesser satisfaction; and her heart may still be attached to her first lover. It is related that Jabir, one of the Companions of the Prophet, married a nonvirgin woman. On hearing of this the Prophet said to him, "Would you not have taken a playful virgin; you would play with her and she would play with you!"

6. Familial respectability should be also taken into account. A man of a respectable family is likely to be more responsible and more trustworthy. And a woman from an honorable origin can be better trusted with the task of rearing her children and bringing them up in a respectable way. A modern poet says:

> The mother is a school; if she is well reared you are sure to raise a noble nation.

7. Marriage between eligible but close relatives, like cousins, is not encouraged. Socially it may lead to disruption of the good relations obtaining within the blood group; and psychologically the familiarity between the spouses might reduce the

degree of sexual excitement between them. It is believed that such marriages produce physically weak offspring.

☞ LEGAL ELIGIBILITY

The most important consideration is legal eligibility—that is, that the would-be spouses should not be of the prohibited degrees of marriage. A prohibition may be either permanent or conditional; and it may be based on (a) blood relationship, (b) marriage, (c) breast-feeding of a baby, or (d) religion.

MARRIAGE PROHIBITIONS BASED ON BLOOD RELATIONSHIP

1. One's own origin: parents, grandparents and so forth.
2. One's own descendants: children and their offspring.
3. The descendants of one's own parents. This category includes siblings: brothers and sisters from father and mother or from father or mother only. It also includes descendants of these and their descendants, and so on. So there can be no marriage between a brother and a sister or between a man and his niece or between a woman and her nephew.
4. The first degree of the descendants of one's own origin beyond the parents. This includes the father's brothers and sisters, the mother's brothers and sisters, the grandfather's brothers and sisters, the grandmother's brothers and sisters, and so forth. Children of these, however, are not prohibited; so the daughter of one's father's sister is eligible to her male cousin from her mother's brother, and so on.

PROHIBITIONS BASED ON BREAST-FEEDING

If a baby, boy or girl, is fed from the breast milk of a wet nurse when it is under two years old, the wet nurse becomes the milk mother of the baby and her husband becomes its milk father. This leads to a series of marriage prohibitions on the same lines of prohibitions resulting from blood relationship. The parents of the milk parents become the baby's milk grandparents, and so forth. The children of the milk parents, either by birth or by milk feeding, become the baby's brothers and sisters, and their offspring are the baby's nieces and nephews, and so forth. However, the prohibition does not extend to the baby's own brothers, his parents or grandparents or the offspring of these. They remain strangers to the baby's milk parents and to their relatives.

However, the prohibition of marriage on account of breast-feeding applies only on the following conditions:

(a) The sucking was from the breast of a living woman, who was at the time of sucking no less than nine years old, the minimum age of puberty.

(b) Sucking should have occurred five complete times. (Short interruption within one session of sucking is disregarded.)

(c) The age of the child at the time of sucking was two years or less. Sucking at a later age is not counted.

PROHIBITIONS BASED ON MARRIAGE RELATIONSHIP

The marriage prohibitions arising from blood relationships or from breast-feeding, as explained above, are permanent. The prohibitions arising from marriage relationships are either permanent or temporary.

The permanent prohibitions as applied to a man are:

(a) The former wife of one's own father or grandfather.

(b) The former wife of one's own son or of a son's son.

(c) The mother of one's own wife (mother-in-law).

(d) The daughter of one's wife, if one's marriage to the wife has been consummated. If separation from the wife occurs before consummation, her daughter is not forbidden to her former husband.

The temporary prohibitions are:

(a) The wife's sister.

(b) The wife's mother's sister (maternal aunt).

(c) The wife's father's sister (paternal aunt).

These three are prohibited as long as the marriage to the wife is continued; but if separation occurs, the prohibition is lifted. (The temporary prohibitions presuppose the permissibility of polygamy, which will be discussed later.)

Corresponding prohibitions apply to a woman. It is clear that the reason for the prohibition of marriage between the above categories of relations is to avoid tensions that may arise from marriage between persons already connected by strong ties involving great mutual rights and obligations. Tensions caused by marriage may break these significant ties.

PROHIBITIONS BASED ON FAITH

Marriage is forbidden:

(a) Between a Muslim boy or girl and an idol worshipper.

(b) Between a Muslim girl and a non-Muslim boy.

A male Muslim may marry a non-Muslim girl who belongs to a religion believed to have been revealed by God and with a sacred book for the guidance of its adherents. These include primarily the Jewish and Christian faiths—"people of the Book" —and the privilege is extended to the Sabian religion and Zoroastrianism, whose adherents attribute to their founders some sort of sacred book and the notion of prophethood.

However, although permission is given to a male Muslim to marry a non-Muslim girl from the above-mentioned background, most of the legal schools regard this practice as undesirable, unless there are mitigating circumstances. This kind of disapproval was the stand of early scholars of olden days, when the Muslim faith inspired awe and respect.

I regard this disapproval to be all the wiser now, in view of our current political and economic weakness (from which I believe we shall recover in due course). A wife from a society which considers itself to be of a higher civilization may very well be less respectful and less faithful to her Muslim husband.

A mitigating circumstance, however, is the anticipation that the girl will embrace the faith of Islam. Another is the fear that fornication will be committed if the marriage is not forthcoming. But if there is a likelihood that the offspring of the marriage will fall under an adverse influence, marriage will be regarded as a prohibited act.

We do indeed endorse the general undesirability of marrying a non-Muslim girl, except in exceptional circumstances in which the girl is apparently in favor of Islam and will faithfully behave toward her husband as a Muslim wife would, and will cooperate with her husband in bringing up the children as good Muslim persons. This is especially so when the couple are to live in a predominantly non-Muslim society. The child of a Muslim is a Muslim by the operation of Muslim law and has to be brought up as such.

We indeed have high regard and great esteem for the West and its civilization; but there are elements in the West of which we disapprove. For example, we are very much opposed to what we regard as moral laxity in the West. We disapprove of the easy mixing between men and women; of the wide circulation of pornographic material; of the custom of dating and of what are euphemistically called "premarital relations." These, in our view, are unhealthy, immoral and destructive. We loathe eating pork and the habit of drinking alcoholic beverages. We dislike the publicity given to the improper activities of libertine movements, and the homosexual demonstrations, and the open unrestrained talk and discussion about these filthy, degrading kinds of behavior.

We also disapprove of resorting to expediency as a means for reaching public office or attaining other objectives, no matter what the moral judgment may be, so long as the corrupt measures are not detected by the legal agencies. We also respect the law, but our compliance is dictated by our conscience and by the moral value of the issue; and we fear God, who is aware of what lies in the breasts of men. We, like any other people, strive for wealth and materialistic gains, but this sentiment in us is balanced by our intense belief in the realities of divine reward and punishment due on the Day of Judgment.

A Muslim cannot just split his character and cannot honestly be expected to tolerate the doing in his house of objectionable acts which are painful to his conscience. For example, if a wife who is not loyal to Islamic values should insist on her freedom to practice something forbidden but to which she is accustomed, domestic harmony will suffer.

Moreover, a wife from the West, with no loyalty to Islam, is apt to think, mistakenly of course, that she belongs to a higher culture and to look down upon the background of her Muslim husband. Seeing that Muslim countries are politically weak and materially less advanced than the West, she may despise the faith of her companion, and transmit these dangerous sentiments to his children.

I was deeply shocked and appalled, when I began my duties in the United States five years ago, to meet grown-up children of a Muslim father who confessed that they were Protestants, Catholics, Baptists or adherents of other denominations. The more the experience was repeated, the deeper my distress became!

I came across these discoveries often during funeral prayer services over deceased Muslims. When the children were introduced to me, and their religion was revealed, directly or indirectly in the course of our conversation, I was amazed! In the beginning I could not believe it. I even hesitated in my mind then over whether I should participate in prayers over a man who condoned the loss of his own children to Islam. The children or their mother or all of them would tell me that the man was such a good Muslim, and so concerned, that he requested that in his death he should have a Muslim prayer service.

I indeed knew better; and it often occurred to me to tell them that if they really cared about the comfort of his soul, they should at least return the children to their legitimate faith in order to save their dear helpless one from the torment of hellfire!

Unpleasant revelations of this type accumulated, and much to my surprise I discovered that some of those who were counted as leaders in the community of Islam were victims of the submissive trend. Some excused themselves on the ground that at the time they married they could not find brides in the Muslim population of America; but they now realize that they could have easily imported suitable ones from home!

Of the couples I have united in marriage, 30 percent were mixed, three were exclusively Christian, and the rest were exclusively Muslim. In the mixed marriages the husbands were Muslims, usually by birth, occasionally by recent conversion. I often enjoy a sense of gratification when I think of the success of the many marriages whose ceremonies I performed between couples of identical faith, and I feel proud of the friendships this happy experience has promoted. It is such a pleasure to encounter the couples again and read in their eyes and on their faces the satisfaction and happiness resulting from deep and real compatibility; and the moment they call at my office with their first baby is an occasion filled with a supreme sense of fulfillment and blessing for all. But I must confess the pain and torment I suffer when a complaint is made to me by either party of those mixed marriages, when the cause in the last analysis is of religious origin!

I must repeat, however, that I am not dogmatically opposed to mixed marriage. I am only cautioning and warning the young male members of our community, in their own interest, that in their search for female spouses they should not surrender easily to passion and what may appear to be convenient arrangements. They should also think of and assess the prospect of a happy domestic life and the children they are to rear. I must also add how proud I was of those grooms who were of such strong and inspiring character as to persuade their brides to seek knowledge of the faith and then willingly and voluntarily ask me to help them embrace the religion of Islam!

☞ DANGEROUS PREMARITAL PRACTICES

In this context we have to warn against the practice of dating and "premarital trials." Potential spouses are not to taste each other prior to the marriage contract by which they become legal husband and wife. If they do, it is fornication; and fornication and adultery are denoted in Islam by a single term, *zina,* as one of the most serious sins against God.

To tolerate fornication among youth as a means for selecting compatible spouses is very dangerous. It may, and it does, lead to conception outside of wedlock, with its attendant evils, resulting in what are now called in the West "unwed mothers" and "fatherless children," who become a great burden on society. Moreover, once the barrier of shyness and the fear of God has been broken, repetition of the experience becomes easier. I wonder what married girls or married boys who went through this "ritual" of trials prior to marriage would feel when they meet their former lovers? And what would the former lovers feel toward them and their spouses and children? It seems to me that the premarital activities could easily be repeated with the former lovers, and with others, when opportunities arose. Since there is no deep sense of shame or fear of God, and the experience with strangers was enjoyed without restraint, what on earth can prevent repetition of these ventures when the eyes of the spouse are not there to see and the agents of the law are not there to check? Mutual trust between husband and wife, the bulwark of domestic stability, becomes shaky; and a silent, permissive resignation may even develop in which each party tolerates the covert misbehavior of the other!

Muslims attach great importance to virginity, and Islam emphasizes the importance of purity of descent. Every child must be born of a known legitimate father; and illegal intercourse, before or after marriage, is strictly forbidden. It should also be severely punished, if it is proven by confession or by four reliable male witnesses. The accuser exposes himself or herself to severe punishment unless the claim is sustained by the minimum number of reliable witnesses.

Let us quote here the following relevant Koranic passages:

> *And go not near fornication. Surely it is an obscenity; and its way is evil and harmful. [XVII, 32]*

> *Surely those who accuse chaste innocent women are cursed in this world and the hereafter; and for them there is a grievous chastisement. [XXIV, 23]*

And the following are traditions attributed to the Prophet, peace and blessings be upon him:

> *Whoever falls in love but restrains himself [or herself] from forbidden acts and resists his [or her] passion, will die as a martyr.*

Each part of the body of the son of Adam can have its [forbidden] share of fornication. The eyes fornicate with lustful looking; the hands fornicate by an undue touch; the legs fornicate by walking [to an evil destination]; the mouth fornicates by an impermissible kiss; the heart fornicates by its evil thought and craving, and the genitals may yield to or may resist the cravings of the heart.

An evil, lustful look is one of the poisoned arrows of Satan. Whosoever endeavors to resist its effect for the fear of God, God will plant in his heart a faith whose sweetness he will enjoyably taste.

In another tradition, which counts seven categories of people who will be protected from the burning heat of the sun on the Last Day, the Prophet said:

And a youth whom a woman of beauty and prestige sought to seduce, but he responded, saying, "I fear God, the Lord of the worlds."

I call upon Muslim parents and urge them, with a sincere heart, to endeavor to maintain their hold upon their children, and protect them from current corrupt practices, and inculcate into their minds the precious moral values of our faith. We agree that there may be a generation gap; and we remember the advice of Imam Ali, the Prophet's cousin, "Bring up your child [prepared] for a time different from yours." But to train them for a different time does not mean to neglect them or to let them become victims of corrupt practices. After all, it is in their own interest.

Chapter Three

Formal Procedure of Marriage

BETROTHAL—"KHITBAH"

The boy having made up his mind and chosen the girl who he thinks will happily fit as his companion for life, a formal betrothal is recommended. The custom is to send word to her father or other senior member of the family, whoever that may be, alluding to the boy's intention and indicating his desire to visit them at a given time in the company of some of his relatives or friends. The girl's family may invite some of their relatives or friends too. When the meeting is held at the agreed time, the boy or his father, brother or friend should reveal his intention, preferably in the following words:

Praise and gratitude are due to God. We seek His help and forgiveness. May He accept our repentance and protect us against evil desires and wrong deeds. Whoever is guided by God cannot go astray and whoever is abandoned by God, no one can lead him aright. I bear witness that there is no god but God and that Muhammad is His servant and Messenger.

I have come to ask for the hand of your daughter [or your sister, e.g.], whose name is so and so, for myself [or for my son or brother or friend, so and so].

The representative of the girl's family may then answer, repeating the same introduction of prayers, and concluding by a word indicating either acceptance or decline.

It is customary to make a gift to the fiancée at this party. The gift used to be some kind of popular food, but nowadays it is generally an engagement ring. Some even exaggeratedly present the fiancée with assorted jewels in addition to the ring.

This formal betrothal is not a legal contract. It does not make the parties husband and wife; they become merely affianced. In fact, betrothal may be omitted altogether and the next step proceeded to directly if the boy is ready; but the betrothal step is recommended as an intermediate stage, binding the two parties in a nonlegal tie. This provides a chance for greater acquaintance, and a period of grace, short or long, in preparation for the next serious stage—the marriage-contract ceremony.

Betrothal is a sort of moral binding. It does not give rise to the right of alimony; and if broken, it does not involve legal consequences, except perhaps the return of unperishable gifts, if the break is not caused by the giver. Of course, it is bad to break the engagement unless there is a very good reason for it.

During the interval between betrothal and the execution of the marriage contract, it is forbidden for any outsider to do anything to undo the relationship. To take the boy away from his fiancée, or to propose to the girl, is strictly prohibited. The Prophet, peace and blessings be upon him, says:

Let not a Muslim ask for the hand of a girl who has been proposed to by someone else.

In this interval gifts may be exchanged, particularly on special occasions, but no unchaperoned contact or private meeting between the betrothed boy and girl should be permitted.

MARRIAGE—CONTRACT CEREMONY— "AQD AN—NIKAH"

☞ ESSENTIAL PARTIES

This is the most important step in the process of marriage.

Once it has been performed, the two parties become legally bound to each other.

The following persons, at the least, should be present for the ceremony: the bride or her agent; the bridegroom or his agent; two male witnesses; or a man and two women. The more witnesses the better.

In Islam the father, and only the father (or, in his absence, the father's father), may give away in marriage his young son or daughter who has not yet reached the age of puberty,* if it is in the child's best interest. The young spouse, being a minor, cannot conduct the marriage contract himself or herself, and the father should conduct it as the guardian.

However, this habit was rarely adhered to in former times; and presently the Muslim states, as do all states in the United States, stipulate a minimum legal age for marriage, both for the boy and for the girl. (New York civil law, for example, prohibits marriage if the boy is under 16 or the girl is under 14, and requires the consent of parents or guardians if the boy is under 21 or the girl under 18.)

The bride may conduct the contract of her own marriage, just as she is free to conduct all other legal transactions. However, it is preferable that her father or someone else deputize for her.

A girl who is of age cannot be married without her approval, which may be conveyed by a shy smile or by blushing or by shedding tears of happiness.

The groom may appoint an agent for his marriage, but this is not recommended.

If both parties to the marriage contract are Muslims, the witnesses should be Muslims too. If the bride is not a Muslim or if both parties are not Muslims, the witnesses need not be Muslims. It is preferable, however, to pick witnesses of reliable character.

---

*A girl attains puberty and becomes a major when she begins to suffer the experience of menstruation; and the boy attains it on having the experience of emission. If the experiences are delayed, they become majors on reaching the age of fifteen lunar years.

☞ FURTHER REQUIREMENTS

The ceremony should be witnessed by as many people as possible in order to publicize the event. Moreover, it is helpful that an experienced, knowledgeable person should conduct the ceremony, to ensure fulfillment of the basic requirements of the contract. In Muslim countries this task is entrusted to a marriage registrar, *ma'dhun,* in each village and in each district of large cities.

In the United States this duty is entrusted to clergymen, to judges in the courts, or to any person granted the power by the state. However, no person, clergyman or otherwise, may perform a marriage ceremony unless he is registered and sworn in by the state.

In addition, the law in the United States provides that the bride and her groom must surrender to the marrying official a marriage license from the state in which the ceremony is to be performed. This license is required even when the parties are in the country on a short visit. Some states, like New York, require a second license when the parties have already been married legally and the ceremony is repeated simply for religious or other reasons. However, the license is easily obtainable on submission of valid blood-test certificates for bride and groom and on establishing their legal eligibility for marriage.

The license must be filled out by the officer or clergyman who performs the ceremony, and is to be returned directly by him to the issuing marriage office within a prescribed short period. But he himself issues a certificate of marriage which he hands over to the united couple. He also must keep a full marriage register at his own office.

In Islam the bride must receive, or at least be promised, a special marriage gift called *sadaq* or *mahr.* The term may be translated as "dower." This dower to be paid to the bride is in no way degrading to her status. It is not a bride price, but a "bridewealth" given to her as a gesture of esteem.

The dower has to be of some suitable value. It can be a gift of money or some benefit, like the use of a house or teaching the bride some useful knowledge such as the Koran. If it is some wealth, such as money or jewels, it may be all advanced or all postponed or partly advanced and partly postponed. The dower postponed in full or in part becomes due on separation by death or divorce. However, if the dower is not specified and agreed upon prior to or during the contract, the bride will have the right to claim a dower commensurate with her status, which can be determined by what was given, for example, to her mother or elder sister.

☞ PLACE OF THE CEREMONY

The marriage ceremony may be performed anywhere—in a house, in an office or in a court. Preferable, however, is a mosque.

☞ CONDUCT OF THE CEREMONY

The Islamic marriage ceremony is very simple indeed. Essentially, it consists of an offer of marriage made by the bride or her agent to the groom or his agent, and of an expression of acceptance by the groom or by his agent. The offer and acceptance have to be made in the presence of witnesses.

There are no further formalities required at all—no best man, no order of entry or anything else. The bride may wear a wedding gown or any suitable other clothing; and she and the groom may sit or stand.

A perfect procedure would be as follows:

1. Witnesses and guests take their seats.

2. The bride and the groom (or their agents,) sit facing each other in such a way as to be seen and heard by the witnesses. They may hold hands, the right hands, symbolizing the unity being established between them. Their hands may be covered by a piece of white cloth.

(In case there are best men and bridesmaids, and so forth, they may take their places as convenient.)

3. When all have settled down in their places, the officiating clergyman stands facing the bride and the groom and their guests, and after greeting his audience delivers the following ceremonial discourse:

Grateful praise is due to the Almighty God, the Merciful, the Compassionate. He created man male and female, each in need of the other, and established the institution of marriage as a means of uniting the two souls in a blessed bond of love, leading to their pleasure and happiness in a way advantageous to mankind. In his Holy Book, our Lord says, "And He it is Who has created man from water; then He has made for him blood-relationship and marriage-relationship. And your Lord is ever Powerful."

And He reminds us of one of His great favors, saying, "And of His signs is this: that He has created mates for you from yourselves that you might enjoy blissful tranquility in their company. He promotes between you love and compassion. Surely there are signs in this for those who reflect."

And He commands: "Give away in marriage those among you who are single. . . . If they are needy, God will give them from His bounty. And God is the most Ample-giver, and Knowing."

And peace and blessings be upon His great and beloved Prophet and last Messenger, Muhammad, who emphatically urged Muslims to marry. He said: "O ye youth! Whoever of you can afford to marry, let him do so. For marriage is the best protection against lustful eyeing and a strong shield for your chastity."

Ladies and gentlemen, at this precious and auspicious moment we are uniting in the sacred bond of marriage, in obedience of the guidance of our Lord and in adherence to the practice of His beloved Prophet, Miss So and So and Mr. So and So, who have decided to live together as husband and wife, sheltered with the blessing of God and His divine Benevolence. May He fill their life with joy and may He grant them peace, health and prosperity! May they always live together in an atmosphere of tranquility and never-diminishing love and tender regard for each other.

4. He then addresses the bridegroom and reminds him of his responsibilities toward the bride, and advises him to be kind,

forgiving and devoted to her; and to provide her with a delightful life under his shelter as strongly taught in Islam. He then turns to the bride and advises her of her obligations toward her husband, and her basic function in the household. He should stress to both the bride and groom their mutual responsibility in taking good care of the children who may be given to them as a gift from God.

5. He then addresses the guests again in such terms as follows:

> *And now, ladies and gentlemen, we are about to listen to our bride and bridegroom giving themselves away to each other in a contractual sacred bond. We all are witnesses to this blissful event. So let us ourselves seek the pleasure and forgiveness of our Lord, the Almighty God. May He absolve our sins. May He accept our repentance. May He guide us in the right path and make us worthy of being witnesses of this marriage.*
>
> *Our Lord! Bless this gathering. Bless us all. Bless our bride and our bridegroom. Grant them health, success and prosperity. Amen!*

6. The officiating clergyman now asks the bride to offer herself to her groom in marriage, and helps her to say to the groom the following words:

> *I offer you myself in marriage in accordance with the guidance and the teaching of the Holy Koran and the Holy Prophet, peace and blessing be upon him.*[1]

---

[1] In case there are terms agreed upon prior to the contract ceremony, such as the kind and amount of dower or that the wife should have the right to divorce her husband, these terms may be specifically mentioned or generally referred to in such words as "and on the terms agreed to between us." The dower is usually written in the marriage certificate issued by a Muslim clergyman. If there are other conditions, they should be added in the certificate.

7. He then asks the groom to address his bride as follows:

I accept your offer of marrying you in accordance with the teaching and the guidance of the Holy Koran and our Holy Prophet, peace and blessings be upon him.[2]

8. The clergyman then asks the bride to address her husband again as follows:

I sincerely and honestly pledge myself to be a faithful and obedient wife to you.

9. And he then asks the bridegroom to say to his bride:

And I pledge myself honestly and sincerely to be a faithful and helpful husband to you.

10. The clergyman then concludes the ceremony with a word of congratulations to the couple and their families, and a word of greeting and a prayer to them and to their guests. A ceremony of exchange of rings may take place then.

When the marriage-contract ceremony has been performed, the couple legally become husband and wife, whether the marriage is consummated immediately or long after.

WEDDING

By wedding we mean the consummation of marriage by the bride and groom upon assuming a common residence. This may be achieved by the bride's going to the home of the groom, or by the groom's moving to the residence of his in-laws, or by bride and groom's both moving to a new apartment or house of their own.

---

[2] Here again, the words "and on the terms agreed upon between us" should be added in case there are such terms.

The wedding may take place on the same day as the marriage-contract ceremony, as appears to be the custom in the United States, or it may be delayed days or weeks or even months. However, from the religious point of view, three things should be observed on the wedding occasion:

1. There should be some sort of entertainment, like beating a drum, music playing and so forth. This is in order to fill the occasion with happy memories for the newlyweds and to provide greater publicity for the event.

2. A wedding feast to which relatives and friends are invited should be held. Acceptance of such an invitation is a religious obligation. Participation in such occasions enhances brotherly feelings, and declining may cause an opposite result, unless there is a legitimate reason.

3. The wedding activities should be conducted within reasonable limits and within the financial capacity of the parties concerned. Moreover, objectionable acts and indecencies should be avoided.

The types of wedding activities have assumed traditionally well-defined forms, depending on the localities. In some countries the festivities take two days, the eve of the wedding day and the wedding day itself. In other countries it occupies many more days, each day having its own ceremonies. A common feature, however, is to call the eve of the wedding day *lailat al-Hinna,* "The Henna Night," and the wedding day *lailat al-farah,* "The Night of Pleasure." During the Henna Night, henna used to be applied to the hands and feet of the bride and groom, still in their own homes. On the wedding day the bride and groom assume their common residence, and the feast party is held in the house of either the groom or the bride, depending on tradition, or in a catering house, as is often done today.

It is a delightful and stirring scene to see the bride's party graciously stepping to the house of her bridegroom, the bride in her colorful clothes and wearing her jewels, and preceded by an entertainment band singing their beautiful songs and playing their enchanting music. Along her way candy or rice is thrown, symbolizing the hope of fertility, or to ward off evil spirits, if superstition is to be believed. If the bridegroom moves to the house of his in-laws, he goes in pageantry escorted by relatives and friends.

Gifts are usually distributed to the guests at the conclusion of the wedding feast, in the form of candy or eggs, beautifully packed or elegantly and deftly wrapped. Guests also, especially relatives and close friends, usually bring presents to the bride and groom.

The bride and groom may not participate in the public feast, as a special meal is to be sent to them in their new private quarters. It is called the Mutual Meal. It is supposed that having this meal together in private, just when they are about to consummate their marriage, brings them closer together and thaws any formalities that may still exist between them.

I still recall my experience of this mutual meal with my bride some years ago. It consisted of very delicious rich dishes. Unfortunately I could not take full advantage of the opportunity, as I had lost my appetite because of the exhaustions of the day. I assumed that this must have been the luck of many bridegrooms like me.

It is to be added that the weeks preceding the wedding day are busy ones for the families of bride and groom—preparing the wedding clothes and wedding cakes, and also in the entertainment at night which may be attended by close friends.

I have observed that many Muslim couples in America have abandoned their traditional wedding customs and adopted the stereotyped Western wedding practices. True, there is nothing inherently wrong in adopting the Western customs so long as no prohibition is violated and extravagance is avoided. I must confess, however, that I was appalled when I attended a reception of this type for the first time. I loathed the appearance of some women who had applied heavy cosmetics and were indecently clothed; and I was astonished to see liquor lavishly served! I hated the sight of women dancing with strange men, close to each other, almost hugging each other, in an ecstatic mood.

This sort of experience has been repeated many times, and

always I have found it dull and even painful. I hate particularly the shouting and the piercing noises of the musicians, and the lack of variety and creativity in the procedure. I also loath the illegitimate public kissing and hugging between strangers of opposite sexes; and the artificial formalities of the men in charge of what they call "chapels" assigned to perform the marriage ceremonies in expensive catering houses, which unduly adds to the apprehension and fears of the already excited bride and groom!

Chapter Four

A Happy Conjugal Household

※

MUTUAL RIGHTS AND OBLIGATIONS INCLUDING SEX ETIQUETTE

In order to ensure an atmosphere of harmony and to promote a cheerful and successful life in the newly established nest of the newlyweds, Islam has provided guidance in defining the relationship between husband and wife and in distributing the rights and obligations arising from this relationship.

In Islam the husband is the head of the household. This is not male chauvinism. It derives from the natural psychological and physical makeup of the male. Man does not suffer from a regular monthly indisposition, with its attendant adverse psychological effects. He does not have to be confined by pregnancy or for delivery; nor can he feed children from his breasts. He is therefore always ready to go out and search for sustenance for himself and his dependents.

In fact, it was Islam which delivered woman from her plight. It established her equality with man both theoretically and practically. It restored her dignity and recovered her freedom. The Koran stresses her right to benefit from the fruits of her efforts as much as man is entitled to benefit from his (IV, 7). It severely condemned the old customs of ill-treating women (XVI, 58/59 and LXXXI, 8/9), and protected their rights in one of the longest chapters, IV, which is given the title "Women." We have already noticed that in the process of the marriage contract, the bride initiates the offer of marriage, a significant detail which emphasizes her spontaneous free action in making this most important decision.

Let us now set out to consider the obligations imposed by Islam upon the husband toward his wife, and then proceed to discuss those of the wife toward her husband.

THE HUSBAND'S DUTIES

1. A husband is responsible for the protection, happiness and maintenance of his wife. He is responsible for the cost of her food, clothes and accommodation. Although she may have to cook, he has to buy her the raw materials and cooking and kitchen facilities, as may be required and applicable. He may also have to buy her two sets of clothes or more each year, providing the types of clothing suitable for the seasons. However, the number of sets of clothes and their quality depend on the husband's means and social requirements. A wife is also entitled to a comfortable, independent accommodation, suitably furnished and provided with basic sanitation facilities. She is not obliged to stay with the husband's parents or relatives as he is not obliged to live with hers. She is also entitled to enjoy herself with her husband in a relaxed atmosphere, free from the embarrassment caused by the presence of another adult in the household.

The cost of smoking or of a forbidden food or drink is not to be provided by the husband.

2. In addition to providing these material needs, a husband has to be kind, understanding and forgiving, and must treat his wife in a tender and loving manner. He not only should avoid hurting her but should bear with her if she ever does something

disagreeable, so long as this clemency does not spoil her and she does not habitually behave out of bounds. The Koran reads:

> . . . and treat them [women] kindly. [IV, 19]

And the Prophet, peace and blessings be upon him, says:

> [Fear] God, [fear] God in the matter of women. They are weak partners, a trust from God with you; and they are made by the divine word permissible for you.

He also says:

> Whoever of you whose wife behaves in a disagreeable manner and he responds by kindness and patience, God will give him rewards as much as Job will be given for his patience.

Patient behavior was the practice of the Prophet, even when his wife dared to address him harshly. Once his mother-in-law saw her daughter strike him with her fist on his noble chest. When the enraged mother-in-law began to reproach her daughter, the Prophet smilingly said, "Leave her alone; they do worse than that." And once Abu Bakr, his father-in-law, was invited to settle some misunderstanding between him and Aishah. The Prophet said to her, "Will you speak, or shall I speak?" Aisha said, "You speak, but do not say except the truth." Abu Bakr was so outraged that he immediately struck her severely, forcing her to run and seek protection behind the back of the Prophet. Abu Bakr said, "O you the enemy of herself! Does the Messenger of God say but the truth?" The Prophet said, "O Abu Bakr, we did not invite you for this [harsh dealing with Aishah], nor did we anticipate it."

3. It is further recommended that a husband be relaxed with his wife, and cheer her up with his humor and by making agreeable jokes. The Prophet, peace and blessings be upon him, in spite of his lofty status, used to play with his wife. He ran in

competition with Aishah. Sometimes she won, and other times he won. And once, hearing an Abyssinian entertainment team playing outside the home, the Prophet said to Aisha, "Would you like to see them?" When she agreed, he sent for them and they came and performed in front of his door. The Prophet stretched his hand, putting his palm on the open door and letting Aisha's chin rest on his arm so that she could see comfortably. A while later the Prophet asked Aishah, "Enough?" She said, "Silence!" Another while later he asked, "Enough?" and the answer was again, "Silence!" But when he asked her for the third time, "Enough?" she agreed, "Yes," and the team went away on a gesture from the Prophet. He then said, "The most perfect belief is that of those who are best-mannered and most tender with their wives." The Prophet also used to say, "Surely God does not love a rough person who is boastful, and rude to his wife." A Bedouin widow once described her husband: "He came always with a smile and left with a greeting. When he was hungry he ate whatever was found, and did not bother when something was missing!"

4. It is of supreme importance that the husband endeavor to handle the matter of sex relations with skill, care and understanding. He should not regard his wife as an object for his own enjoyment alone but as a partner with whom he should seek mutual bliss, satisfaction and fulfillment. He should always approach her with love and tenderness. In the early stages of marriage, especially in their first experience on the wedding day, he has to be particularly gentle.

The husband should always have due regard for his wife's feelings and should endeavor to let her reach the degree of full satisfaction in this respect. Because of the importance of this element, early Muslim authorities discussed such details as love play, the techniques that arouse excitement, and the question of orgasm. The rich Islamic literature treating this subject far exceeds and is more original and stimulating than—but not so obscence as—the crude and vulgar material now in wide circulation in the West. We may discuss here some of the remarks made by these early authorities.

They stress the importance of preliminary love play—caresses, fondling, kissing, endearing words—in order to arouse the wife's sexual passion and prepare for a deeper sensation and a successful conclusion.

At the beginning of actual coitus, it is recommended that the following prayer be said:

In the name of Almighty God, the Most High. Please, God, ward off the evil forces away from us and from the blessings You bestow upon us.

The authorities also recommend that in the process of coitus, especially before full penetration, the excitable areas of the female genitals be gently provoked to contribute to complete fulfillment.

We have to remind the reader, however, that even at this moment of absorption and ecstasy, propriety and cleanliness have to be maintained. On the one hand, both partners may utter exclamations or ejaculations venting or expressing the intensity of their pleasure, which also may increase the degree of their excitation; but neither may scream to the degree of disrupting the natural privacy of the act. Some Companions of the Prophet, peace be upon him, recommend the repetition of the words: *Allahu Akbar*, "God is Great."

On the other hand, it is to be remembered that the liquid (lubricating) material discharged by the sex organs on excitement is counted as a pollution and a polluting element in Islam and that a Muslim is forbidden to smear a part of his or her body with a polluting stuff unnecessarily. Therefore the custom of licking the excitable areas with the tongue said to prevail in the West may not only be unhealthy; it is also forbidden on that account. We also feel that it is indeed disgusting; and this disgust might in the long run plant the seeds of hatred in the hearts of the couple and ultimately break their relationship.

The position to be assumed by male and female in relation to each other during coitus occupied a great deal of the attention of Muslim authors who treated the subject. They compiled some fifteen basic different positions; and within each choice they suggest varieties of details. We do not need to discuss this matter here at length, since husband and wife, in their search for their own fulfillment, can easily discover these varieties and select what they find to be most suitable and comfortable for themselves.

Muslim writers also emphasize that the husband should endeavor to achieve mutual orgasm. If he should fail to hold out sufficiently for his partner, they say he should continue his efforts to have her reach a climax. To rush away from her too soon might be injurious.

They also recommend that parting at the end of the act should be slow, pleasant and cordial, not abrupt or indifferent.

After some rest both parties have to have the full ablution (a bath). This duty does not need to be rushed; but when the time of the next prayer comes, it has to be performed to remove the ceremonial pollution arising from coitus. Prior to having this bath, the parties, like a woman during her period of menstrual discharge, are forbidden to perform prayers or to touch or read the Koran. Moreover, it is better to delay hair-cutting and fingernail-clipping until after the ablution.

It is also recommended that the husband seek to introduce changes and variations in his approach and in the performance, even in little details, in order to avoid boredom. Variations also create a sense of novelty, and novelty stimulates interest and curiosity; and this intensifies the feeling of pleasure and enjoyment.

These Muslim etiquettes are probably best summed up in the following words attributed to the Prophet:

> *Let not one of you fall upon his woman in the manner a male animal suddenly jumps over its female victim. Let there be a messenger [to go] between them."* He was asked, "What is the messenger, O Messenger of God?" He said, "Kissing, and endearing speech.*

Another tradition reads:

> *Three practices are shortcomings in a man; namely, to fail to enquire about the name of a man he has just encountered, but was worthy of friendship; to refuse a favor extended to him in good faith; and to assault his woman without introductory entertainment [to stimulate her], and so he satisfies his own desire before she can achieve her own fulfillment.*
>
> *When one of you retires with his wife, let them not strip off their cloths completely in an animal-like manner; and let him begin by [stimulating her by the use of] fine exciting speech and by kissing.*

In the course of their game of pleasure a husband and his wife may enjoy and fondle any part of the body of each other; and their engagement in this kind of activity is regarded as a type of divine devotion. However, a husband is discouraged from looking at his wife's genitals, perhaps for its adverse psychological effect. Moreover, coitus is strictly forbidden during the menstrual period; and penetration in the back passage is always forbidden. If the female genitals are to be avoided during the menstrual period, presumably because of their temporary blood pollution, a filthier pollution is an eternal factor in the case of the back passage. Prohibition also applies to all types of unnatural and unproductive activities, whether committed between two persons of the same sex or otherwise.

Early Muslim authorities also discussed the advisable frequency of coitus. Some advised that the experience should be repeated at least once every four days. It seems, however, that the matter of frequency should be left to the mood and personal inclination of the parties concerned, which indeed depend on many factors, including their age and the condition of their health.

5. A husband should also see to it that his wife has sufficient knowledge of her religious obligations and encourage her in observing her devotional duties. Of special importance are the

rules pertaining to the menstrual period. During this period, as well as during the period of postnatal discharge, the obligation of mandatory prayer is lifted; and coitus is forbidden. The prohibition of coitus is lifted when the blood discharge has stopped and the woman has had the ablution of a full bath.

6. A husband should not harbor doubts or suspicion about his wife unduly. Jealousy is indeed a natural element; and a husband is not to be too indulgent or to remain indifferent in reasonably provocative situations, and surely must guard his wife against all corruptive influences. Yet he should not allow fanciful thoughts to engage his mind and should not behave in a spying manner toward his wife. The Prophet, peace and blessings be upon him, said:

> *There is a type of jealousy which God loves and there is another type which God hates. As for that which God loves, it is the jealousy which is provoked by a legitimate cause of suspicion; and that which God hates is the jealousy which is unduly aroused.*

The Prophet once asked Fatimah, his own daughter, "What is best for a woman?" She replied, "That she should not mix with men and men should not mix with her." The Prophet, who was pleased with her answer, hugged her and said, "An offspring resembling its roots."

Thus a happy life depends on mutual trust between the partners; and all that has to be done is to keep away from situations that are likely to incite evil or arouse suspicion.

7. Tension often arises between people living contiguously, and it is bound to arise between husbands and their wives. It was emphasized above that a husband should be indulgent, forbearing and forgiving; but a wife may become unbearably obstinate. In this case her husband should strongly advise and warn her. If this proves to be ineffective, he may resort to some light punishment. This may take the form of withholding some favors he is accustomed to extend to her, or turning his back to her in his sleep, or sleeping separately from her. If these

measures should yet be ineffective and he thinks that beating her might bring her to her senses, it may be allowed for the sake of rescuing the otherwise threatened family life. However, he should not beat her severely, and should never beat her on the face.

Now, it may be wondered what a wife should do if her husband behaves unjustly toward her. Can she in turn beat him? No. It would be inconsistent with her femininity to behave in a rough manner. In fact, her tenderness and love would probably be her most effective weapon. No reasonable husband would fail to bow and even melt under the tender appeals of a loving, faithful wife. She should also deliberate within herself whether her husband's attitude may not be her own fault. May she have failed to take care of herself so as to appeal to her husband? But if she realizes that it is indeed the fault of her husband, she may then ask for a council made up of a representative from her side and a representative from his side, to consider the dispute and make peace between them. If the domestic dispute becomes chronic and the cleavage appears to be beyond repair, whether it is the fault of the husband or of the wife or of both or of neither of them, but the experience of living together has proven that they are incompatible, and continuing the relationship is intolerable, the solution may be dissolution of the marriage, which will be discussed in a later chapter.

8. If the wife becomes pregnant, her husband should display greater consideration for her and should do all he can to alleviate her discomfort. When she is delivered, he should be grateful to God for her safety and for what God has beneficently graced them with. If his wife has been delivered of a male child, he should not go out of his way to show his pleasure; and if it is a female, he should not at all feel disheartened. After all, he does not know which is better for him. The Prophet, peace and blessings be upon him, says:

> *Whoever is graced with a daughter and treats her well and lavishes upon her some of the favors God has bestowed upon him, she will be a protection for him against the punishment of the Hell Fire.*

Whoever brings home some good thing to his children, it will be counted as a divine charity for him. Let him begin by giving the female ones. Whoever cheers up a female child shall have the merit of him who weeps out of divine fear of God; and whoever so intensely fears God, God will protect him from the Hell Fire.

Whoever has two daughters or two sisters under his care and treats them well, he will be my companion in Paradise.

A child, however, should be given a good name, even if it is delivered in a miscarriage. And shortly after a child's safe birth, the full text of the call to prayer should be recited in its right ear, and the short one in its left ear. It is recommended that a boy be circumcised on the seventh day of his birth, excluding the day of birth itself. Whether it is a boy or girl, it is recommended that the family then hold a feast for which a lamb or larger animal should be sacrificed. Some of the meat should be distributed to the poor, as well as the value of gold whose weight is the weight of the baby's hair. The sacrifice offered on the seventh day of birth is known as *'aqiqah.*

THE WIFE'S DUTIES

1. The first task of the wife is to create at home a soft, relaxing atmosphere in which she and her husband can live together smoothly, happily and enjoyably. The way in which this is to be achieved depends on her taste and their means and upon prevailing values and conditions.

2. A wife must be faithful and devoted to her husband. Her loyalty is due to him first, even before her kin. She should avoid associating with undesirable or suspicious elements and should not entertain alone any male friends.

3. The management of the household is the wife's primary responsibility. She has to take care of meal preparation, housecleaning and laundry. Whether she undertakes these tasks her-

self or has them done under her careful supervision, it is her
task to manage them in the best interests of the family. She may
expect some cooperation from her husband, but this should
depend on what he can afford to do. What is important is the
mutual goodwill and love which will no doubt stimulate each
party to alleviate the burden of the other as much as possible.

4. The wife should not be too demanding; she must be con-
tented, and appreciative of any kind gesture her husband may
extend to her. She should not insist on buying expensive clothes
or luxurious pieces of furniture beyond her husband's means.

5. The wife should take care of herself in order to appear
always cheerful, charming and attractive to her husband. She
should always smell good and may reasonably apply cosmetics
but should avoid excessive use of it. Such excess is not only
financially unwise but also psychologically harmful. It makes
her beauty appear to be merely artificial. An ancient Arab woman advised her daughter on her wedding day:

> *O my daughter! You are leaving the home in which you
> were brought up to a house unknown to you and to a com-
> panion unfamiliar to you. Be a floor to him, he will be a
> roof to you; be a soft seat to him, he will be a pillar for
> you; and be like a slave girl to him, he will be like a slave
> boy to you. Avoid inopportune behavior, lest he should be
> bored with you; and be not aloof lest he should become in-
> different to you. If he approaches you, come running to him;
> and if he turns away, do not impose yourself upon him.
> Take care of his nose, his eye and his ear. Let him not smell
> except a good odor from you; let his eye not see you except
> in an agreeable appearance; and let him hear nothing from
> you except nice, fine words.*

6. In managing the household, the wife should economize
and avoid extravagance. She is not to give of her husband's
wealth except within the degree he approves of. Whatever she
gives within this degree, she will share in its divine reward;
and what she gives away beyond it will be to the advantage of

her husband and to her own disadvantage on the Day of Judgment.

7. A wife should regard the conjugal home as her own castle; and she should not leave it except in the company of her husband or with his specific or general approval. Much will depend on prevailing conditions and customs; and an intelligent, honest wife can easily and intuitively make her sound judgment in each situation. It is related that a wife who leaves her home without permission from her husband will be cursed by the angels until she returns.

Husband and wife are closely bound to, and deeply interested in, each other. Therefore each has the right to know specifically, or at least generally, depending on the circumstances, the whereabouts of the other when he or she is absent from home.

8. When she goes out for a legitimate reason—shopping, visiting or to a job approved by her husband—the wife should be dressed decently and should walk and behave in a dignified manner. She should avoid making an exhibition of herself along the way or in the marketplace, and should cast down her eyes, as men also must do. The Koran reads:

> *Say to the believing men that they should lower their gaze and restrain their sexual passions [against commission of prohibited acts]; this is purer for them. And God knows what you do openly and what you hide. And say to the believing women that they should lower their gaze and restrain their sexual passions and not display their adornment except to the agreeable and normally appearing degree; and let them spread their covering over their bosoms . . . and let them not strike [the ground] with their feet [in walking] to attract attention to what is hidden of their attraction. And turn to God all, so that you may be successful. [XXIV, 30, 31]*

9. A wife should be pleasant, respectful and obedient to her husband. A family, simple or complex, is a team; and the hus-

band is its natural head, responsible for its protection and welfare. His wife is to cooperate with him, and the type of her cooperation depends on the degree of her education, training and general ability and health conditions. During the period of her menstrual discharge, during her pregnancy and during the postnatal confinement, she is not to be unduly burdened with work.

It is probably because the husband's capability is not periodically checked or interrupted by menstruation, childbearing, confinement or breast-feeding that God has installed him as head and put him in charge of the family. In this respect the Koran reads:

> *Men are in charge of women, because of the degree men are granted over women, and because of their financial responsibility. [IV, 34]*

The degree given to men over women alluded to here is not a degree of preference of men over women in the eyes of God, since the Koran, which has established the equality of the sexes, cannot contradict itself. It does allude to the biological differences which impose upon the male partner the task of leadership of the household.

Although Islam has assigned to the husband the responsibility of the full maintenance of his household, wife and children, and has given the wife the right to depend entirely on her husband for all her needs and the needs of her children, yet husband and wife may agree on any domestic arrangement within the obtaining social framework. In our time, for example, the cost of living has risen considerably; and it has become customary for women to undertake part-time or full-time paid jobs. For example, if the husband's income is not quite sufficient for the domestic needs, and the wife, without compulsion from the husband, is willing to engage herself in a job acceptable to her husband in order to contribute to the maintenance of the family, this will of course be unobjectionable.

We may remark in this context that Islam regards that recognized customs and prevailing traditions are to be taken into consideration in assessing the validity of human behavior, so long as they are not at variance with the basic moral values and are not opposed to Koranic teaching.

10. Although she should devote her paramount attention and loyalty to her husband, a wife should also remain loyal and attentive to her parents and other relatives. The husband, too, while his wife and children are his first responsibility, is still obligated to be kind and helpful to his parents and relatives, even if they belong to a faith different from that of his choice. Each party should also be cordial and friendly with the relatives of the other. Let us quote here some relevant words from the Koran:

> *And We have enjoined on man concerning his parents— his mother bears him with weakness over weakness, and his weaning takes two years, saying: Give thanks to Me and to your parents. To Me is the eventual return.*

> *And if they strive with you to associate with Me that of which you have no knowledge; obey them not but keep kindly company with them in this world. [XXXI, 14, 15]*

> *And serve God and associate nothing with Him; and be good to the parents and to the near of kin and the orphans and the needy and the neighbors of [your] kin and the alien neighbor. [IV, 36]*

> *And give to the near of kin his due and to the needy and the wayfarer, and squander not wastefully. [XVII, 26]*

The Prophet, peace and blessings be upon him, was also asked, "What is the most meritorious act?"

"Observing the prayer duty in its appointed time," the Prophet said.

"And what is next?" he was asked further.

"Kindness to the parents," the Prophet replied.

"And what is next?" he was asked still further.

"The struggle in the way of God," he said.

It is also better that each of the spouses should feel not only like a member of a closed, isolated small family unit but also like a significant member of a larger group united by blood and marriage ties. It is more reassuring for a girl to feel that while she is protected by her husband, there are also others who, if a disaster should occur, will come to her rescue and take care of her and of her children, not because of a cool, formal and corruptible legal obligation but because of deep personal affection and sincere concern stemming from real and effective ties of relationship with recognized mutual duties and obligations. It is psychologically not sufficient to feel dependent on a small household, and on a vague, huge, indifferent membership in a state in which interrelationships are based on a coldblooded, impersonal law. Physical isolation of the small family is a mental isolation and loneliness for its members who may seek outlets in unhealthy immoral deviations in the absence of the protective elements of the larger family.

Let us now quote some interesting traditions relevant to the obligations upon the wife toward her husband, attributed to the Prophet Muhammad, peace and blessings be upon him:

> *A woman who observes the mandatory prayers and the fasting of the month of Ramadan, and preserves her honor and obeys her husband, shall be rewarded in Paradise.*
>
> *A woman is nearest to her Lord [God] when she is in the inner part of her home.*
>
> *A woman who dies while her husband is pleased with her will be among the people of Paradise.*
>
> *If I were to command a person to prostrate to a mortal, I would have required the wife to prostrate to her husband in view of his great rights upon her.*

A woman said once to the Prophet, "I am an unmarried woman and wish to get married, but I need to know what rights a husband has over his wife." The Prophet, peace be upon him, answered:

> *It is the right of the husband over his wife that she should never deny him her favors whenever he approaches her. It is his right that she should not give away anything from the household without his permission. If she should do so, she will bear the consequences and he shall get the divine reward [for the gift]. It is his right that she should not fast [voluntarily] without his permission. If she does, she will only suffer hunger and thirst without a reward. And if she goes out of the house without his permission, the angels will curse her until she returns, unless she repents.*

Let us quote also the following advice given by a poet-husband to his wife, who both lived in early times:

> *Accept the least from me cheerfully and gratefully; my love to you shall be everlasting. And argue not with me when I am overcome with temper.*
>
> *And beat me not, the beating of a tambourine; you do not know what is to come thereafter.*
>
> *And do not be of a complaining nature; as frequent complaining may cause love to dwindle; and my heart may begin to be detached; it is in the nature of the heart to change.*
>
> *I see that love and injury cannot dwell in one heart together; wherever injury comes to reside, love would soon part.*

An objective analysis of the above outline of the mutual rights and obligations of husband and wife as set out and stipulated by Islam for the guidance of its adherents reveals the following facts:

1. The husband-wife relationship is to be based not on dry legal rules or decisions of the court but on mutual respect, love and regard.

2. The husband is alone responsible for the entire cost of, and the wife is the mistress of, the household. The objective of each is to serve the other and to provide to the other means of comfort, enjoyment and happiness; and the aim of both is to achieve optimum bliss for themselves and to contribute through their offspring to the perpetuation of the human race.

3. A woman is not a chattel or a blind follower but an equal partner. However, her soft nature, her beautiful natural role as the partner who is to provide more for the sexual attraction and excitement, her monthly menstrual discharge with its attending psychological and physical adverse effects, her childbearing and child-rearing—all these natural considerations, not a male dictatorship as has recently been contended, have made her the dependent but respected, virtuous and beloved partner.

4. Within the framework of the above basic considerations, and within the Islamic flexibility which has regard for custom and prevailing traditions, consistent with the moral values of Islam, the couple may choose any type of arrangement for the distribution of their mutual responsibilities in order to meet their needs as they may see fit in the conditions prevailing where they live.

5. An interesting point which emphasizes that the wife does not lose her own independent character on getting married is that she always retains her full maiden name. So Miss Nancy Jones on her marriage to Mr. Martin James is called Lady Nancy Jones and not Mrs. James. She may be called Lady Nancy Jones, wife of Mr. James, but not simply Mrs. James. This point is significant, as it expresses both the wife's greater freedom under Islam and her continued relation with her own family.

Chapter Five

Birth Control and Abortion

BIRTH CONTROL

Birth control means "to seek to regulate the frequency of birth and reduce it to the desired number through obstructing human conception by chemical or mechanical means."

Long before the development of modern science and the discovery of the concepts and functions of the sperm and the ovum and the subtle details of fertilization, humanity had hit upon the idea that the male discharge into the womb of the female was a prerequisite for conception, although people entertained divergent interpretations of the hidden process of fertilization. In other words, early society realized the necessary role of the male discharge in the process of conception and knew that isolating it from the female genitals would prevent pregnancy.

Early society, however, had had no serious ecological reasons for taking deliberate measures to reduce its population. On the contrary, it was more desirable and even prestigious for a family to have a large number of children. Children were economically useful and militarily helpful.

Yet the practice of blocking the way of conception seems to have taken place in early times, though rarely and sporadically, for immoral or for social reasons. Adulterers who feared that pregnancy would reveal their illicit relationship, and men who copulated with concubines or with wives from whom, for one reason or another, they did not wish to have children, apparently attempted to prevent conception in the simple manner which was obvious to them.

This method seems to have been known and practiced among the Arabs on a small scale at the time of the rise of Islam. There are some traditions that speak about it; and in one of these traditions the Prophet, peace be upon him, seems to discourage it, saying, "No soul God has decreed to exist except that it will exist." The term used for this practice was *azl*: isolation of the male liquid discharge from the place of fertilization by withdrawing at the moment of reaching the stage of orgasm.

In our sophisticated modern age, with the great leaps in the field of medicine and widespread education and use of hygienic methods, resulting in a sharp reduction in the rate of infant mortality and in lengthening the average life expectancy, ecologists, economists and statisticians have become alarmed by the threat of what they call the "population explosion." The only remedy, they seem to think, is to curb the rate of birth; and medical scientists came to their help by devising several chemical and other methods for the practice which has become known as birth control. Now this question has become of great concern to religious leaders, to social reformers, to governments and to the United Nations. Some governments, like that of the United States, allocate huge funds for birth-control efforts and stretch their campaign to a global scale.

The agitation for the practice of birth control has led to a great controversy, as the practice seems to work against the deeply rooted social norm calling for larger sizes of tribal population; or, as it seems to some, it works against the will of God when that will is about to plant a life; or, as it seems to others, it amounts to the crime of murder. The Catholic church, led by the Pope, has taken the lead in resisting the movement and condemning it, while other denominations have argued against the prohibition.

What is the attitude of Islam toward the policy and the practice of birth control?

We have just quoted above a tradition which seems to discourage the practice of *azl*. The wording of the tradition is important in two respects. On the one hand, the text as it stands, "No soul decreed by God to come to life except that it will come," does not describe the practice as murder, which it is not. The concept of murder presupposes a human life already existing; and life in the unfertilized sperm is by no means a full human life. On the other hand, the tradition appears to mean that the act of preventing fertilization in this manner is also decreed by God, since if fertilization was decreed nothing could prevent it. A point worth noting here is that tradition seems to have been said in the context of the undesirability of the practice of *azl*, as it amounts to denying a wife complete fulfillment of her climax by the sudden withdrawal from her when she is on the point of reaching her orgasm. This indicates that the wishes and the decision of the wife have to be taken into consideration.

From all the above, we may conclude that the practice of *azl*, or any of the similarly harmless methods of birth control, though it is not encouraged, is not prohibited either, so long as it is engaged in by the mutual consent of husband and wife.

It is interesting to quote here the opinion and argument in this respect of a great and widely known Muslim authority, Al-Ghazali, who died in A.D. 1111, more than eight and a half centuries ago. In his famous work *The Revival of the Sciences of Religion*, he says:

> *The jurists are divided over the question of the practice of azl. There are those who believe that it is unconditionally permissible; there are those who maintain that it is always forbidden; and there are some who say that it is permissible on the condition that the wife agrees to it. It appears that those of the third opinion pay greater attention to avoiding hurting the wife than to the idea of azl itself.*

In our own opinion, it is permissible, though it is better not to practice it. It is as much as a man is sitting in a mosque silently instead of engaging himself in good readings or in prayers; or like a person living in Mecca who does not perform pilgrimage annually [after performing the mandatory obligation].

We do not subscribe to the opinion prohibiting it because a prohibition has to be based either on a clear divine text or on a firm foundation of analogy. There is no [such text nor an] analogical foundation; but on the contrary, there is an analogical basis for permissibility; namely, the unprohibited idea of bachelorhood, abstention from copulation, and holding back ejaculation during copulation. These are similar to azl and are not prohibited, although they are not recommended modes of behavior.

The formation of the fetus depends (not forgetting the role of the will of God) on four stages; namely, marriage, copulation, continuing copulation until the moment of ejaculation, and remaining until the discharge settles in the womb. These four causes are similar, and abstention from one of them is like abstention from the others. This is unlike abortion or killing one's own child by burying it alive [a practice existing with some ancient Arabs, and condemned and stopped by Islam], because the latter is a capital crime against an already existing human life. . . . The child is not created from the male semen alone before it mixes with the water of the wife. . . . As much as the child is not created from the male semen when it is still in the vertebrae of the male, it is also not created after ejaculation unless it mixes with the woman's water or blood. This is the clear analogy.

If you argue, Would you not regard it, azl, at least as a disapproved act in view of the evil intention to prevent the possibility of the birth of a child? I would say there are various intentions which may accompany this practice; and it depends on the type of the intention.

Al-Ghazali then proceeds to count these intentions and give

his ruling regarding each case. Let us quote the following interesting part:

> *One of the possible motives for this practice is the intention to preserve the beauty and the voluptuousness of the wife for its greater enjoyment, or to protect her life and spare her from the pangs of birth. Neither of these intentions is prohibited.*
>
> *Another intention is the fear of hardship that may be caused by [supporting] the needs of a large family, and the evils such hardship may entail. This is not forbidden, although it is better to trust to God and depend upon Him. As God states: "And there is no living creature walking or creeping on the earth except that on God is its sustenance" [chap. XI, 6]. It is analogous to the permissible saving of wealth for future needs, which is not consistent with the notion of absolute dependence upon God.*
>
> *Another motive is the fear of bringing forth female children for the hardships the problem of their marriage may cause; an attitude similar to that of some ancient Arabs who used to bury alive their female babies. This is an extremely evil motive; and the practices arising from it, including prevention of birth by any means, including abstention from marriage, are forbidden.*

We agree with Al-Ghazali in regarding the motive of the couple as the factor which basically determines whether the practice of birth control is permissible or not.

At the top of the list of evil motives which make the practice strictly prohibited, we should put the desire of a couple to carry on an illicit relationship without being exposed to the disgrace or the hardships of pregnancy. But when a couple have a legitimate cause, and birth control is carried out with mutual consent, without undue suffering or harm to either party, the practice should be regarded as permissible. This is like the case of a couple who already have a number of children and fear deterioration of the wife's health through further pregnancies and births, or who fear the greater hardship of providing for the cost of confinement and of bringing up more children when the cost of living is very high.

I am not, however, in favor of mechanical sterilization of a healthy woman or of a man. I regard such operations as immoral and degrading, especially in the case of the male. It may be justifiable, however, in the case of a woman whose health is really threatened by the possibility of pregnancy and birth.

While we agree to the practice of birth control in limited legitimate cases when it is harmless to the couple and is done with their mutual consent, we strongly oppose its universal application as a matter of a general policy within a Muslim group or country when such a policy is unwise in a given context. I would not preach it as a recommended general principle to Muslims in the United States, for example, where an increase in their number would be advantageous to their faith. And in a country where the political or military strength of the Muslim element derives from their number, the adoption of the practice of birth control as a government policy is injurious to Islam. Examples of such a situation are not difficult to find in countries of the Middle East and Far East.

ABORTION

"Abort" means to "terminate the life of the fetus deliberately, by any means, while it is still in the womb of its mother."

Abortion, although it has in common with birth control the notion of curbing the frequency of successful birth, is sharply different in that it is murder of the already existing life of the fetus and is a danger to its mother. It is therefore generally regarded as being under serious prohibition in Islam.

Early Muslim jurists were familiar with the fact that the fetus in the womb of its mother undergoes certain stages of growth, although the details which they learned from their anatomists of the process of fertilization and what follows were somewhat crude. Associating conception with cessation of the menstrual discharge, they believed that the fetus was created from the menstrual blood held up inside the mother. The male semen, however, was necessary, they said, because when it mixed with the female liquid it caused it to coagulate and to become a fertile milieu for the growth of the fetus. Thus the function of semen in human fertilization, they said, resembled that of rennet in the process of turning milk into cheese.

The notion that the fetus grows and develops in stages was derived from the Koran, which reads:

> *And certainly We created man from an extract of clay. Then We made him a small life-germ in a firm resting place.*
>
> *Then We made the life germ a clot, then We made the clot a lump of flesh, then We made [in] the lump of flesh bones, then We clothed the bones with flesh, then We caused it to grow into another creation. So blessed be God, the Best of Creators.* [XXIII, 12/14]

A widely known tradition attributed to the Prophet speaks of the period of the three early stages of the fetus in the womb, and says that the fetus remains first as a drop of pure liquid for forty days, and then becomes a clot for another forty days, and then becomes a lump of flesh for another forty days; and then the *ruh*, the spirit of life, is blown into it.

Some jurists interpret this literally and regard the fetus as lifeless for the first 120 days. Basing their opinion on this assumption, they regard abortion during this early four months of conception as permissible, but disapproved unless it poses a real danger to the life of the mother.[1]

Other jurists disagree with this opinion and condemn abor-

---

[1] It was an interesting coincidence that shortly after this was written a report appearing in the New York *Times* (2/11/70) under the heading "Shifts Unlikely in Abortion Law," stated, "A number of legislators have proposed an even earlier deadline confining legal abortions to the first 12 weeks of pregnancy."

tion at any stage as a serious prohibition, amounting to the murder of a human life, although they agree that the crime assumes greater proportions when abortion takes place at an advanced stage.

However, if the life of the mother becomes really threatened by the continuance of conception, according to the advice of reliable experts who regard abortion as the only way to rescue her from this danger, abortion then becomes permissible, as it is likely to save one of two threatened lives.

Under no other circumstances is late abortion allowed. We do not see, even in the case of rape, any element to justify it. The raped girl is the innocent victim of a brutal aggression, and her conception should bring no disgrace to her whatsoever.

The permissive laws recently introduced in some states have been flagrantly abused. They open wide the gates for adulterers and fornicators who find in them an easy solution to their illegitimate pregnancies and an encouragement to their immoral pursuits. They also give the greedy a chance to enrich themselves from these bloody immoralities. According to recent reports, 69,000 abortions have been performed, or rather, 69,000 innocent babies have been legally murdered, in New York City alone in seven months, from July 1970 to January 1971; and at least one agency serving as abortion-referral brokers between physicians and pregnant girls, chiefly unwed, has accumulated $1 million in fees! And so thousands of babies are daily murdered unduly; morality is continuously and openly butchered unashamedly; and big money is greedily grabbed undeservedly. And yet the conscience of the world is unperturbed! May God preserve us, Muslims, from this contagious and inhuman genocide!

Churchmen and government agencies must abandon their permissive attitude, for the sake of the nation's prestige and of society's moral health, and for the sake of humanity at large. The concept that morality is dynamic must be abandoned. The inherent moral value of an act does not change with time. Nor would widespread violation of a moral principle in any way violate its legitimacy or call for reforming it. What was forbidden to Abraham and Moses is forbidden to us. Robbery is still robbery, and murder is still murder, and fornication is still fornication. When sodomy became widespread among Lot's people, God did not alter its character as an evil act; we know what God did to those people! The Koran relates the story in the following brief manner:

> *And [remember] Lot when he said to his people: "You commit an abomination in a manner unprecedented by anyone in the world.*
>
> *"You indeed come to males with lust, instead of females. Verily you are a people exceeding the bounds."*
>
> *And the answer of his people was no other than that they said, "Turn them [Lot's family] from your town; they are a people who aspire to purity."*
>
> *So we delivered him and his followers, not including his wife who was of those who remained behind.*
>
> *And We rained upon them a rain; see, then, what was the end of the guilty! [VII, 80/84]*

It is shameful indeed to speak openly of 20 million professed homosexual Americans! May Almighty God guide all to repentance and to assuming a decent and chaste life!

I am extremely perturbed by the shameless open demonstrations by homosexuals and by the audacity of some corruptive writers who stand to defend this "gay liberation" movement, seeking to argue that homosexuality is not unnatural, not immoral and not a sickness. Leaving aside the argument over whether it is or is not a disease, we strongly hold, against the argument of Michael Kotis,[1] that homosexuality is unnatural and immoral. It is unnatural, not only because it is unproductive but also because it is perverse. It forces one of the participating parties into the manner and psychology of the opposite sex. The male sufferer takes on a soft, effeminate attitude, unnatural and inconsistent with his physical and psychological

---

[1] "Homosexual Militance," New York *Times*, 2/19/71.

makeup; and the aggressive woman artificially wears harsh male garb, forcing it onto her otherwise soft, feminine nature! The Prophet, peace and blessings be upon him, cursed women who behave like men, and men who behave like women.

Traces of homosexual behavior claimed to have been discovered in some odd primitive societies are no evidence of a historical human homosexual trait. Anthropologists are the last to derive a history from a contemporary human behavior. From the above-quoted Koranic text, it appears that sodomy was invented by the people of Sodom. It is dangerous to misuse anthropological findings, to strip them of their context and employ them for deceiving analogies. The inherently indisputable evil and filth of homosexuality for its own sake make it incomparable to such disputable institutions as polygamy, which is digestible in some cultures and indigestible in others.

To claim that homosexual relations between consenting parties are moral on the ground that they bring joy to the partners and no harm to others is inadmissible. Is not the male sufferer hurt and his male character destroyed by his perversion? Does the homosexual act really manifest "a selfless loving concern for another person"? Or does it manifest a selfish concern for one's own misplaced lust? What about the effect of homosexual behavior upon the spouse, children and relations of the homosexual? Where is the wife who would be glad to learn that her husband is being used, assaulted and enjoyed as a soft, effeminate creature by other males? And where is the tolerant husband who would cherish the idea that his wife was being prostituted by other women one way or another? What about incestuous homosexual or heterosexual behavior between consenting adults? Using the same argument, a daring author might advocate its morality.

To my mind, a mode of behavior is moral if it becomes socially beneficial, or is at least harmless if it should be universalized. Just imagine that in one generation all men became sodomites and all women became lesbians, and there were no heterosexual marriages. What would be the effect on mankind?

Let us now turn to abortion in relation to the desire to check the rapid increase in populations. I say that if we are to regulate population growth and guard against the dangers of population explosion, indiscriminate abortion is not the answer. Our first and foremost measure should be to hold fast to virtuous behavior and rid ourselves of promiscuous practices. This would automatically cancel the birth of millions of unwanted babies. And a second important measure is the cultivation and promotion of a real and sincere human brotherhood. The world has become too small for national rivalry, racial prejudice or imperialist domination. Richer countries should share their material and scientific wealth ungrudgingly with countries lagging behind. And healthy family-planning measures should be undertaken in an international spirit of genuine cooperation and mutual help.

Chapter Six

Polygamy

❦

The practice of polygamy is perhaps the feature best known in the West about Islam. Early European travelers exaggerated exotic cultural phenomena unfamiliar at home, which caught the imagination of their readers. But there is always danger in passing judgment on a cultural trait in isolation from its context.

Social scientists apply the term "polygamy" both to the practice in which a woman is married to more than one husband, which they call "polyandry," and to the more frequent practice in which a man is married to more than one wife, which they call "polygyny." I use the term polygamy here in the latter sense.

Early human society realized the danger inherent in the practice of polyandry, and it was therefore rarely applied. The danger lay not only in the severe competition that would arise between jealous husbands but mainly in the confusion over determining the fatherhood of the children. That danger does not arise in the practice of polygyny. It also seems that the interruption of the female sexual capacity during the monthly and postnatal menstrual periods and the lack of such interruption in males had something to do with the greater frequency of polygymy.

Islam, it is true, permits polygamy; but Islam does not encourage it. Under no circumstances is a husband permitted to have five or more wives, which was not uncommon before and at the time of the rise of Islam. And marrying more than one wife is conditional upon the anticipation of a faithful application of the principle of justice between co-wives. The husband's time and attention must be truly shared, and any gesture or action that might provoke the jealousy of a wife must be avoided. If the husband of two wives goes on a journey, he must take them both with him or leave them both at home. If he can take one only, she must be chosen by drawing lots; and the next journey must be the turn of the other. The Koran eloquently stresses this duty by warning the husband contemplating another marriage in the following words:

> *But if you should fear that you will not do justice, then confine yourself to one wife. [IV, 3]*

This, however, may appear to the Western reader to be a strange arrangement and an insult to the dignity of the woman. In our view, it is not. If it is degrading to the woman, why does she herself agree willingly to be a second wife? It is strange to us to condemn this practice in an organized and limited manner and at the same time tolerate the adulterous patronization of women by husbands under the so-called monogamous system. Is not this illicit or explicit "concubinage" more degrading to the woman, and to the man too?

I solicit the indulgence of the reader and draw his attention to the fact that this liberal legislation of Islam is made against a restrictive background of psychological, social and economic factors. The human inclination normally confines a man to mating with one spouse; and the fear of the tension at home which is bound to arise from bringing in a co-wife, and the financial burden involved, are safeguards against uncontrolled frequency of polygamy. Moreover, the Koran guards against the abuse of this liberalism by warning:

> *And indeed you cannot do justice between women, even when you are eager to be [completely just]. [IV, 129]*

And thus this Islamic liberal legislation, combined with the restrictive social and natural factors, as well as the stress on the principle of justice between wives, which is difficult to apply, has produced a limited and balanced flexibility which has provided healthy outlets in compelling situations in which a husband has to take another wife but cannot part with the first one out of compassion or for other reasons. Political advantage and the sterility of the first wife were the most frequent factors leading to polygamy, which has always been the rare exception.

A relevant question which may arise here pertains to the marriages of the Prophet Muhammad himself, peace and blessings be upon him. At one time he had nine wives in his household. In our modern time, critics of the Prophet find in this theme an opportunity to vent their hatred of the Prophet, and accuse him of oversensuality, an accusation which stems either from ignorance or from deceitful malice.

A critic of the Prophet in this respect has to answer certain questions before passing a condemnatory judgment: How old was Muhammad when he became polygamous? What were the circumstances in which each of these polygamous marriages took place? What was the degree of physical attraction of each of his polygamous wives? Did he ever marry after the Koranic legislation limiting polygamy to four wives? And when this legislation came down, why did he retain those above the number of four?

It should be remembered that the Prophet was married first at the age of twenty-five to a widow, Khadeejah, who was fifteen years older, and remained with her alone until she died, when he was fifty. At that time he and a small band of people who followed him were struggling against severe persecution waged against him by the pagans of his home town, Mecca, since his prophetic mission started ten years earlier. Three years later he emigrated to Medina, where he had a substantial following. One year before emigration he married, but was not wed to, Aisha, the young daughter of his foremost supporter and first Companion, Abu Bakr. Subsequent to this betrothal, he was married to Sawdah, a Muslim who had been widowed with dependent children in most distressing circumstances; and one year after the emigration his marriage to Aishah was consummated.

Historians and social scientists recognize the political significance of marriage which forges fresh ties bringing about mutual tribal obligations of protection and help; and Muhammad in his new town had become the political head of the newly born Muslim state, which badly needed protection and support. The political element was clear in his marriage to Aishah, and the compassionate motive was perhaps of greater weight in his marriage to Sawdah.

Over the next six years a series of other political or compassionate marriages to widowed women were concluded; one year later the limitation was established, and women married in excess of the rule were divorced. The Prophet, peace be upon him, was alone exempted, because of the political consequences and the unspeakable misery which would have been suffered by the women condemned as divorcees of the Prophet! This harmless exemption was a great blessing for Islam. These ladies, better known as Mothers of the Faithful, having enjoyed a longer stay with the Prophet, later transmitted to his nation an immense treasure of their experiences in the Prophet's household which has added to the sources of guidance for his followers.

The narrow liberalism of the law of polygamy in Islam was hardly abused by Muslims. Its application has been very infrequent, except in circumstances where local traditions call for it. Moreover, Islam gives the state the right to legislate rules which may at some given time narrow down the degree of freedom granted by the faith in the interest of society. No one questions the government's right to limit driving to one side of the road, or to forbid parking in certain places, or to prohibit the import or export of certain items, or building above a certain height. In the same way the legislature of a state may, if it is in the interest of its people, enact a law forbidding bigamy, a law which may be repealed after a war resulting in an excessive surplus of women, to protect them from descending to the most degrading profession.

Chapter Seven

Dissolution of Marriage

The marriage tie is not only a legal binder but a sacred bond uniting husband and wife in a perpetual relationship, reinforced by mutual love and passionate and tender sentiments which grow in depth and in magnitude with time. This blissful matrimonial bond is further intensified by the birth of children, who become the prime concern of the couple.

All these factors ensure, in most cases, the continuity of marriage and the stability of the family. Domestic stability is further ensured by the guidance of Islam in what the couple should observe and how each should act toward the other, as set out in chapter 4.

INCOMPATIBILITY

The stability of marriage, based on the above factors, is the normal expectation and almost the universal realization. Yet some couples may discover, they think, that they are after all incompatible. However, they should not rush to this conclusion. If tension arises, each should try to be understanding and patient with the other and at the same time should examine his or her own attitude and see whether that may be the underlying cause of tension. If the dispute becomes chronic and the atmosphere unbearable, they are advised to call a representative from the side of each party to arbitrate and try to make peace between them. The Koran reads:

And if you fear a breach between the two, appoint an arbiter from his people and an arbiter from her people. If they both desire agreement, God will effect harmony between them. [IV, 35]

The arbiters should try to reconcile the couple to each other. They are to conduct the case discreetly to avoid embarrassment that may arise from the publicity involving private details. That is why each is to be from among the people of each party of the couple, or at least should enjoy his or her trust and confidence. The arbiters' ruling should be binding, and if necessary, enforced by the court.

DIVORCE

If the arbiters fail to reconcile the couple, divorce then may be the last resort. Divorce is described by the Prophet, peace and blessings be upon him, as a thing most hated by God. The Prophet also said: "A woman who asks for divorce without legitimate grounds will never taste the smell of Paradise." Those involved in a case of domestic dispute should do their best to salvage the marriage before thinking of divorce. If the rupture is irreparable, divorce may then become the inevitable, necessary evil in the interest of the couple.

There are also causes which would recommend the dissolution of a marriage. A husband who realizes his impotence or becomes impotent, or a husband who becomes incapable of bearing the maintenance of his wife and fears that she may fall into immoral behavior, should seek a divorce; and if he does not, his wife has the right to seek a divorce from him. Either party should seek a divorce also on finding that the other party fails habitually to perform religious duties, like mandatory prayers and fasting, in spite of his or her counsel. Otherwise the resort to divorce should be avoided so far as possible.

PROCEDURE

Divorce in Islam traditionally does not involve a stringent or long protracted procedure. Moreover, it does not always require the mutual consent of both parties but if necessary can be effected by the court in the face of an objection by the other party. It is unhealthy to hold to a legal but otherwise broken marriage for too long. This may lead to miseries and maladjustment of the children. Divorce is then better and healthier both for the spouses and for the children. Divorce does not need a prior period of separation.

The minimal procedure of divorce is that the husband, who is a major and in sound mind, pronounces a statement clearly indicating his intention to part with his wife, such as "I divorce my wife," or "My wife is divorced," or "I divorce you," addressing his wife. The wife may not make this proclamation, unless she had demanded and was granted in the marriage contract the right to divorce her husband. If she did not, she may obtain divorce on good grounds through arbiters in the manner described above. If the husband disagrees and she feels justified in her demand, she may apply to the court. The reason the wife is given less say in divorce is probably that a woman is usually more susceptible to emotional pressures, and might misuse the right, if unconditionally given to her, in a situation of temporary emotional distress and then regret having done so when it was too late.

The grounds for divorce in Islam, however, are more liberal than in the West where they are limited to proven adultery, cruelty, and long separation. The Muslim couple may apply for divorce simply when they realize that they cannot live together happily, for any reason. This does not by any means reflect on the stability of the Muslim family. The complex web of ties, social and psychological, are a strong safeguard against rash decisions.

---

1 Judy Klemesrud, "Separation: The Worst Status of All?" New York *Times*, 2/16/71.

Therefore, in practice, divorce has always been the exception. Its relatively greater frequency in recent times in some parts of the Muslim world has resulted from rapid, disruptive social changes which rocked the social order, and the upheavals which accompany such series of shocks.

The current official procedure of divorce usually involves a marriage registrar who represents the court in divorce cases. All the couple have to do if the methods of reconciliation have been exhausted is to go to the government official and the husband pronounce divorce in front of him. The official records the divorce in his register and issues a divorce certificate on payment of a small fee. Some Muslim states nowadays stipulate somewhat a long court procedure for divorce to slow down the divorce rate.

TIMING

Jurists call the interval falling between two menstrual periods a "period of purity", as opposed to the period of menstruation.

If divorce has taken place, it has to be after a period of purity during which there has been no copulation. It is forbidden to divorce a woman during her menstruation, and during a purity period after copulation. Jurists account for this prohibition on the ground that the prohibited timing would unjustly lengthen the period which the wife has to wait before she is entitled to remarry. The waiting duration is three purity periods, including the purity period in which divorce takes place if it was free from copulation. So divorcing her during a purity period after copulation or during a menstrual period would increase the duration of her waiting.

In my own mind there is another important reason. A woman during her menstrual period normally is not at her best either physically or psychologically. At this time, she may appear less attractive to her husband, and he thus becomes less interested in her and consequently less tolerant with her. She may also become impatient and easily irritable. If divorce is rushed in this situation, the couple may later regret it. If they wait, they may be able to mend their misunderstanding. Moreover, in a pure period during which copulation has occurred, it is too unkind and thoughtless of a husband to repay his wife's favors with divorce.

☞ REVOCABLE AND IRREVOCABLE DIVORCE

When divorce takes place for the first time in the above manner, it does not become absolutely final until the expiration of the waiting period. Any time during the waiting period, the couple may decide to rescind the divorce and resume their matrimonial relationship. But if they wait until the expiration of the waiting period and wish to rejoin each other, a new, full contract ceremony has to be performed.

Now, if a divorce occurs a second time, it is also revocable in the same way. But if it should occur a third time, it becomes absolutely irrevocable. The divorcees may not at all remarry unless the wife happens to marry someone else after the expiration of her period and is thereafter separated from this other marriage by death or divorce after it has been duly and fully consummated.

And so the first and second divorces are revocable and the third is irrevocable. The wisdom of making the first and second divorces revocable is not far to seek. After complete separation by divorce, each party may begin to relax and remember the good things about the other. They may regret the separation and resolve to resume their former relation. So the period of waiting is like a period of grace, in which the couple still have a chance to reconsider their decision. However, if no decision is made until the expiration of the period, the couple cannot resume their past except by a fresh contract. The couple is given the chance twice, but not a third time. The aim of stipulating an intervening consummated marriage for the resumption of their relationship after the third time is to make the chance for this resumption after a third divorce further remote, and to impress upon the couple that they should be careful before deciding upon divorce.

☞ POST-SEPARATION WAITING PERIOD

The waiting period is the time a wife has to wait after separation from her husband by death or divorce before she can remarry. Its aim is not only to determine whether she is pregnant from her former husband before she remarries, and thereby guard against confusion of the paternity of the child, but also to give the woman an opportunity to relax and somewhat forget her former associations. It is also more seemly that the woman not jump from the arms of one man into the arms of another too soon.

The period of waiting of a pregnant woman, separated by death or divorce, comes to an end upon the end of pregnancy, whether the period happens to be long or short.

The waiting period of a nonpregnant woman separated by death is four months and ten days.

The waiting period of a divorced nonpregnant woman is three menstrual periods. If she is beyond or below the age of menstruation, her waiting period is three months.

The waiting period of a widow is longer than that of the divorcee probably because the widow needs more time to recover from the shock of her husband's death.

☞ ALIMONY

A divorced husband has to pay for the full maintenance of his revocably divorced wife for the full waiting period. During this period she is still treated like almost his wife. Therefore any proposal of marriage to her during this period, even by allusion, is forbidden.

An irrevocably divorced woman has the right to her full maintenance if she is pregnant, for the duration of her period of waiting. If not pregnant, she has the right to the cost of her accommodation only.

A widow has a right of accommodation only (from the estate of her deceased husband) for the duration of her period of waiting, whether she is pregnant or not.

A hinting proposal of marriage during the waiting period to a woman irrevocably separated from her husband by death or by a third divorce is permissible; but a direct proposal is not. The idea is to maintain courtesy to the former husband and not to provoke his jealousy unduly. On the other hand, the divorced husband has to show sympathy and consideration toward his divorced wife. He should not reveal a secret or attempt to disgrace her in any way. In addition, it is recommended that he send her a good financial gift to help her out during the period of the ordeal of the divorce.

☞ CUSTODY OF THE CHILDREN

The mother who is not incapacitated by a mental, moral or religious cause has the first right to custody of her child, boy or girl, until the child reaches the age of seven, when the right of custody reverts to the father. The father has to maintain the child until such time as he can manage by himself if a boy, or gets married if a girl. A girl does not have to earn her own living. Her maintenance is the duty of her father, and when she is married it becomes the obligation of her husband.

The mother's prior right to the custody of her child is dependent on certain conditions. She must be of sound mind and good moral conduct. She forfeits her right if she is morally lax or pursues a mean profession, such as that of a bar waitress or a striptease dancer. Some jurists stipulate that she must be a Muslim. However, if it is feared that she would bring up the child as a non-Muslim, or might feed him pork or take him along to church, for example, her right to custody is forfeited. She also loses this right if she marries anyone other than the child's father.

If the child's mother is dead or married to a stranger, the right of custody goes to her own mother, the child's maternal grandmother if she is qualified. If there is no qualified mother or mother's mother, custody goes to the child's father. In his absence custody goes to his mother or his mother's mother. In the absence of the child's mother and father, and their mothers and mothers' mothers, custody goes to the nearest female relative, and then to the nearest male relative. If there is none, the court trusts the child to a trustworthy guardian.

A guardian in custody of a child, even if it is the child's own mother, should be paid by the father for her services, including breast-feeding.

When the father is in custody of his child, the child's unqualified mother should be allowed visiting privileges.

Epilogue
Liberation of Women by Islam

The yardsticks by which female freedom is measured in modern times are these: The constitutional right to vote and to occupy public office, and her liberty to adopt revealing modes of dress and to play around with boyfriends, which may lead to fornication and the birth of illegitimate children or to liberal abortion practices.

True female freedom does not have to be manifested in such glamorous or immoral practices. Her freedom, according to Islam, lies in the recognition of her balanced equality to man, in her right to tender protection at young age, her right to choose her future partner, her right to earn and own the fruit of her labor, her right to be treated with dignity, her right to loving protection by her husband, her right to conduct her own business, her obligation to protect her chastity, her right to worship, her freedom to express her opinion in words or in writing, her freedom to make decisions affecting her life, her freedom to exercises her talents, her freedom to lead and, in general, her right to equal treatment based on her equality with man. Individual freedom, however, be it that of a male or a female person, has to be such as not to encroach upon the freedom of others or upon the interests of society.

I certainly have no intentions of making any kind of a detailed comparison between what Islam did for women 1,400 years ago and the brutal treatment of their sisters in Europe at that time, where conferences were held to consider whether a woman had a soul or whether she was a human being. Readers are too familiar with the historical and recent treatment of women in the West, including the harsh punishment meted out to helpless women summarily accused of witchcraft, the deprivation of female children from inheritance, and the denial to women of the right to conduct transactions independently or to possess real estate.

Islam 1,400 years ago affirmed the equality of women to men and made them subject to the same obligations and responsible for their own deeds. It gave women the right to develop their talents and to conduct their own affairs, including contractual transactions, independently from their husbands and fathers. It made a woman free to choose her own spouse, and she could do that as soon as she became of age.

A female's majority, like that of the male, is achieved when she attains the age of fifteen at the latest, but she may attain it earlier, on having the experience of menstruation. She is entitled to hold a public post to which she is qualified; and no complaint has been heard from female employees in a Muslim land of unequal pay on the grounds of sex. A woman, like a man, has to dress decently. The institution of wearing a veil in some lands is a local custom, and its widespread use stemmed from historical factors, not necessarily from the legal or theological aspects of the faith. Muslim women have held leading posts, including ministerial offices and even governorships, both in early and in modern times.

Islam has emphatically urged kind treatment of daughters and made their maintenance a duty of their father until they marry. After marriage the maintenance of the wife becomes an obligation on the husband. And so a woman does not have to work for her living. A son has to seek his living as soon as he can do so. Moreover, a woman has a share in the estate left by her father, in the estate of her brother and in the estate of her husband, if she survives them. It is true that her share is half that given to her brother, but we have to bear in mind his greater financial burden. A mother inherits one-third of her son's estate if he dies childless and without brothers or sisters; otherwise she takes one-sixth.

We have discussed at length the kind of treatment due to a woman as a wife. As for the kind of treatment accorded to her in Islam as a mother, it is superbly recommended in the following examples:

Once a man asked the Prophet, peace and blessings be upon him, "Who is first worthy of my kind treatment?" "Your mother," the Prophet answered. "And who is next?" the man asked. "Your mother," the Prophet replied. "And who is next?" the man repeated. "Your mother," the Prophet said again. "And who is next?" the man asked. "Your father," answered the Prophet.

And the Koran reads:

And We have enjoined upon man to do good to his parents. His mother bears him with trouble and she brings him forth in pain. And the bearing of him and the weaning of him is thirty months. [XLVI, 15]

And your Lord has decreed that you serve none but Him, and do good to parents. If either or both of them reach old age with you, say not even the exclamation of exhaustion in front of them, and speak to them only generous words.

And lower to them the wing of humility out of mercy, and say, "My Lord, have mercy on them as they brought me up [when I was] helpless!" [XVII, 23/24]